THE TOUGH GCSE WORKBOOK: SCIENCE

UNIADMISSIONS

ISBN: 978-1-913683-60-3

Very boring section. Do not read unless you are very
    Very
            Very
                    Very
    Bored

Copyright © 2022 UniAdmissions. All rights reserved.

No part of this publication may be reproduced, stored or transmitted in any form or by any means, electronic or mechanical, including photocopying, recording, or by any information retrieval system without the prior written permission of the publisher. This publication may not be used in conjunction with or to support any commercial undertaking without the prior written permission of the publisher.

Published by *RAR Medical Services Limited*
www.uniadmissions.co.uk
info@uniadmissions.co.uk
Tel: +44 (0) 208 068 0438

Interior grid designed by vectorstock (Image #10070206 at VectorStock.com)

About Us

Hi! We're UniAdmissions. We're a group of students and university nerds who spend all day, every day, trying to help people in classrooms all over the UK get better grades. UniAdmissions currently publishes over 130 books all focused on helping you get the best grades possible in your exams, and getting you into your dream schools and unis. We've been working for almost a decade to bring great books to young people all around the world.

Based in the UK – we always make sure our books are bang up to date with all of the exam boards. You'll always get the highest quality help from us, and the best value for money. What's better… have you got any questions about our books? Any questions about your exams? Any questions about trout? We're just an email, live chat, or phone call away at www.uniadmissions.co.uk

As well as books, UniAdmissions also has a top-notch teaching and coaching team – where teachers, tutors, and other experts run special courses and provide 1-1 private lessons.

With a team of over 1,000 experts (boffins) and a proven track record (we love watching lines go up on graphs), UniAdmissions have quickly become the UK's number one admissions company.

We hope you love our book – we certainly loved making it.

The Tough GCSE Workbook: Science

Contents

GCSE Science Mastery Techniques 6

How To Revise: Mastering Study Tools & Techniques 7
    Task vs Time-Focused 7
    The 'Learning Styles' Myth 9
    The biggest criticisms of the Learning Styles model include:
    10 Awesome Revision Tools & Techniques 17
    So, what does all of this mean for you? 32

Where You Study: The Perfect Study Environment 43
    Social or Solitary Preferences 43
    The Perfect Personal Workspace 44
    Music & Background Noise 45
    Minimising External Distractions 48

When You Study: Finding The Perfect Study Time 54

Tough GCSE Science Questions: 58
    Balancing Equations 61
    Chemistry Calculations 63
        Formulas you MUST know: 65
Biology questions 69
Chemistry Questions 103
Physics Questions 135
Answers 165
    Biology Answers 165
    Chemistry Answers 184
    Physics Answers 206
Final Advice 233

TOUGH GCSE WORKBOOK: SCIENCE | REVISION TECHNIQUES

GCSE Science Mastery Techniques

Welcome to the Tough GCSE Workbook for Science. Inside you will find hints and tips, as well as *tons* of practice questions and answers. Those questions are going to be one of your key revision and learning tools, but the other one is holding this book. You. Revision, and results, have got to come from you as much as anything else – and we're gonna help you do it.

How?

We'll start off with a bunch of special skills, and exam advice – you can use this to take control of your revision, which you can also boost using school text books and any notes you may have taken in lessons. They're next up in this book. Once you've worked through all of our techniques, and you've used our exercises to practice being a revision and learning master, you can hone your skills using our super-tough GCSE science questions and answers.

Without any further ado, though it is probably a good idea to take a look at everyone's least-favourite part of exam preparation: revision. Revising effectively is crucial to performing well in ALL of your GCSEs, particularly in the sciences – as remembering all of the techniques, principles, and knowledge taught throughout your time at school can be relevant.

What we're giving you here, as a result, is a kind of primer. A guide. We've talked to a bunch of boffins about revising and condensed their findings on the *cutting edge* of education science (that's learning about learning, to you and me) into this chapter. We'll introduce you to some tried-and-tested study tools and techniques that can optimise your learning and productivity, revolutionise your revision process and put you firmly on the path towards top grades.

There are three components to this section.

- **How** To Study (learning methods and techniques)
- **Where** To Study (location and surrounding environment)
- **When** To Study (time of day)

How To Revise: Mastering Study Tools & Techniques

Task vs Time-Focused

One of the key factors to consider when identifying our ideal studying style is whether we're **task-focused** or **time-focused** when we approach tasks.

Task-focused individuals will work as long as it takes to complete a task, even if it means falling behind schedule. Once they are in the groove, they are hard to stop. However, it can take discipline to get to work in the first place — and sometimes just as much discipline to stop! It's important for them to define *specific start times*, but also to consider the *latest finish time* they can afford for each task. This will enable them to keep to their plan and avoid falling too far behind because they spent too long on a single task.

Time-focused individuals will set a timer for *x* hours to complete a task, and will then try to complete the task in that specific time period. This sounds effective and well-organised, except that they may also get distracted by WhatsApp messages, Snapchat, and other distractions during this time – and *still* consider it as part of the time they spent working on that task! Techniques such as the Pomodoro Technique are often helpful in allowing them to manage their time more effectively. Setting *realistic time-scales* for task completion and *minimising distractions* is essential to their success.

Neither of these two styles is right or wrong, but it's important to be aware of the advantages and potential pitfalls of each.

Think of the two styles as two ends of a spectrum. Even though we might identify with a few aspects of both, we often have a natural tendency to one over the other. Once we're aware of where our tendencies lie, we can work to ensure that our **planning system** has a way of *accounting* for the potential pitfalls that we might face. We can also begin to experiment with our less dominant style in hopes of combining the benefits of both styles to aid us in our studying.

> **Activity 1.1:** Are you more of a time-focused or task-focused worker? What can you do to prevent yourself from falling victim to the pitfalls of your dominant type?

The 'Learning Styles' Myth

Some of you may have been introduced to the idea of 'Learning Styles' in school; if not, it's possible that you may be exposed to it in the future. The Learning Styles theory suggests that we have individual preferences that determine how we learn best, and that we should be taught using our preferred 'style' in order to maximise our learning. However, scientific studies are becoming increasingly *critical* of this idea.[1]

Before we discuss better alternatives to Learning Styles, it's useful to get a basic understanding of what they are. There are many different categories of Learning Styles, but most include some variation of the following:

1. Learning according to **sensory preference**:

For example, a **visual learner** has a preference for images, pictures and spatial understanding. Useful study methods to learn content would include:

- Mind-maps, pictures and other visual system diagrams.
- Using colour pens and highlighters to emphasise words or concepts.

An **auditory learner** has a preference for sound and music. They may benefit from:
Listening to sound recordings related to the content being studied. Reading notes out aloud, for example with dramatic voice intonations.

A **kinaesthetic learner** has a preference for using their body, hands and sense of touch. They may benefit from:
Using physical objects that can be touched, felt or held, e.g. flash cards, notes.
Focusing on the sensation of pen on paper when writing notes.

2. Learning according to **thinking style**: 'concrete' and 'abstract' learners.

Concrete learners prefer to use explicit facts, data and examples when solving problems. They think practically and logically before attempting to solve the problem, and then approach the problem using well-established methods. When being introduced to new content, they benefit from knowing even the smallest details to ensure that there are no gaps in their understanding.

Abstract learners prefer to use intuition and imagination when solving problems, and they apply concepts and rules in a more fluid way. They may take ideas or observed patterns from one domain and attempt to apply it to a different problem. They may also be able to draw analogies and relationships between concepts that others may not notice.

3. Learning according to **speed** and **accuracy**: 'impulsive' and 'reflective' learners.

Impulsive learners are characterised by being able to solve problems quickly, but inaccurately. They *believe* that they grasp concepts quickly and skilfully, but often take shortcuts when processing new information and end up overestimating their capabilities. With practice, they learn to solve problems quickly and accurately, though their accuracy may still be less than *reflective* learners.

Reflective learners tend to solve problems slowly, but with greater accuracy. Although they may initially take longer to process new content, they're also more likely to spend time and effort understanding the information in order to apply it competently. Reflective learners have often been linked with possessing perfectionist traits.

Having read through the Learning Styles outlined above, it's likely that some of us can see ourselves being portrayed quite accurately in their descriptions! So, why have Learning Styles gathered such a negative reputation amongst the scientific community?

The biggest criticisms of the Learning Styles model include:

No correlation with learning: The Learning Styles refer to traits and tendencies we have as individuals, but there has been no scientific evidence to support that these significantly influence how we *learn*. While Learning Styles were originally adopted from other theories in human cognition, they are being *incorrectly applied* to learning.[1] For example, though someone may have a kinaesthetic preference for perceiving the world (i.e. they process the world more through their feelings and sense of touch than, for example, what they see or hear), this doesn't mean that they are going to be a 'kinaesthetic learner'.

Neglecting skills that come less naturally to us: By concentrating on just one or two preferred modes of learning, we neglect to improve our other cognitive abilities. Instead of just focusing on our strengths, we should devote time to developing the skills that may come less naturally to us. This helps us to enhance our cognitive abilities as a whole and gives us a wider range of tools to solve the different problems that we will be exposed to throughout our lives.

Nature of subject material is more important than individual preferences: A 2006 study showed that different groups being taught the same material performed better when taught using one specific Learning Style.[2] This led to the conclusion that the nature of the *subject* being taught is *more important* than students' individual learning preferences. This makes sense – for example, Mathematics may be easier to learn through practising example questions as opposed to listening to tapes on how to solve a problem. In contrast, Spanish grammar may be easier to learn through reading and making notes compared to drawing pictures and diagrams.

Defined inconsistently, identified inaccurately: There are too many ways to describe Learning Styles (over 71 different styles according to a review published in 2004).[3] Not only are definitions inconsistent across different Learning Styles models, but there has also been criticism directed towards the questionnaires being used to help students to identify their individual learning preferences. Questions may be phrased vaguely and misunderstood by students, leading to answers that don't reflect their preferences.

As a result, the Learning Style recommended by the questionnaire may not be accurate for the student. In addition, any initial bias that a student has towards what they *think* their preferred Learning Style is can influence how they answer questions. As such, the result may simply confirm their initial belief about their Learning Style, even though their performance may prove otherwise.

Given this, what best practices can we draw by integrating the criticisms of the existing Learning Styles model with new developments in learning theory?

1. **Multi-Sensory Approach to Learning**

Instead of focusing on learning via one sensory mode, we should look over the content we're trying to learn using a *combination* of different sensory modes.[4]

One of the most popular examples of this is *dual coding*, which involves combining verbal materials with visual materials.[5] Presenting the same information both verbally (e.g. written notes) and visually (e.g. diagrams, infographics, charts, timelines) gives our brain two different ways of remembering it.

The more creative we get with the visual materials we design, the more likely we are to remember the information that is being described. Combining this with more-detailed text reinforces the content that we're trying to learn and allows us to recall it with greater ease and accuracy.

During studies, when revising by reviewing the 'dual-coded' notes you've created, it may be even more helpful to involve a *third sensory mode* – the *auditory* sense. If you speak the notes aloud, varying your volume and tone as you review them, many people memorise content more effectively than if they were just re-reading the notes they had written.

2. Subject-Focused Learning

As mentioned, the nature of the *subject* being taught is actually more important than students' individual learning preferences.[2] We should consider what methods of learning may be best-suited to each subject before incorporating our own individual studying preferences. Some examples of subject-specific studying techniques that have worked for us over the years include:

Notes combined with visual diagrams (dual-coding); reading notes aloud when reviewing; self-testing with flashcards for formulae and key definitions; Past-Paper questions; explaining each step aloud as if I was tutoring another person.

We recommend that you experiment with applying different revision techniques to different subjects to discover what works best for you.

There will be more information on how to get the most out of revision notes and past-papers in the next section of this chapter (10 Awesome Study Tools & Techniques).

3. Competency-Based Learning

Whether we have a *concrete* or *abstract* 'thinking style' shouldn't be used to inform how we learn. Instead, we should consider how *competent* we are at the subject or module in question. When we're exposed to a completely new and unfamiliar concept, it may benefit us to focus on developing our understanding of the *concrete* facts and methods that form the foundations of that concept. The more familiar we become with the fundamentals, the more capable and competent we become, and we can then begin to experiment with applying our knowledge in an *abstract* way.

In other words, concrete and abstract do not show two distinctive preferences, but instead, reflect our level of expertise at a certain point in time. We should begin as 'concrete learners' when we're a novice or beginner, and then shift to 'abstract learners' as our competency reaches an advanced or expert level.[4]

4. Developing *All* Cognitive Abilities

Instead of just focusing on our natural strengths (as the Learning Styles model promotes), we should devote time to developing the skills that may come less naturally to us. As well as having benefits in studying (e.g. multi-sensory approach to learning is more effective than single-sensory learning), it also helps us to enhance our cognitive abilities overall.

This is invaluable as we make the transition from formal education to the 'real world', where having a wider range of well-developed cognitive skills can help us to solve the problems we encounter (whether in the workplace or in everyday life) in a more practical and effective manner.

To take advantage of this, we first need to identify our natural preferences for learning and problem-solving. In doing so, we can then become aware of the areas that need developing. It's then up to us to make a conscious decision to work on improving these abilities.

> **Activity 1.2:** Think about what your natural tendencies are for how you prefer to learn. Which other cognitive abilities should you develop to help you study more effectively? For each subject you study, which learning methods do you want to experiment with?

10 Awesome Revision Tools & Techniques
Here is a collection of ten of the most effective studying techniques and tools that we have personally attempted over years of studying, and informed by scientific tests and recent research. A few of them are hybrids of existing expertise which we have combined into more effective tools.

1. The Ultimate Revision Note Guide
In all honesty, making revision notes can be a boring and time-consuming process. Most of us don't really know *how* to make effective revision notes, and we end up getting *less* out of them relative to the amount of time and effort we put into making them.

Not ideal at all.

But when done correctly, making revision notes can be an incredibly powerful studying tool. Let's start with the basics.

Hand-Written Notes vs Typed Notes
Studies have shown that hand-written notes are more effective than notes which were typed on a keyboard or touch-screen.[6] The hand movements involved when writing unique letters and forming words is beneficial to learning. The act of writing leaves a

'motor memory' in the sensorimotor part of the brain, which helps a person to recognise letters and strengthen the connection between what is being read and written. This connection doesn't form as strongly when notes are typed, as each letter on the keyboard/touch-screen has the same 'feel' to it.

Most of us associate typing notes as being quicker than writing notes by hand. Although this is good for completing or reviewing topics in a short amount of time, it isn't conducive to learning. Researchers propose that the additional time taken to hand-write notes promotes learning, as more time is being spent on the task and the brain has more time to process the content being written.[7]

Producing large amounts of typed-notes by copying from a textbook or transcribing verbatim from a lecture or lesson has also been shown to be comparatively less beneficial for learning purposes than creating hand-written notes.[7] Even though they may be very detailed, typing notes in this manner can lead to 'mindless transcribing' of information, where more attention is being paid to the typing process than to the content itself.

Finally, if we're doing a written examination, writing notes during our studying preparation can help us train our 'writing muscles' and improve our 'writing stamina'. Great for those essay papers!

Kam's Note-Making Secrets

Kam Taj is an revision expert who honed his skills transforming his grades just like you when preparing for his GCSEs. He has some specific advice here in the guide – but also has a whole book – The Ultimate Guide to Exam Success – if you want more!

My approach:

I performed best in exams where I had made detailed hand-written notes on the topic. I used dual-coding (written and visual content) to remember the content more effectively. I would use different coloured pens and highlighters as necessary to categorise content (e.g. formulae in red, definitions in blue etc.) or to emphasise specific words.

I would re-read the notes aloud when reviewing them, often varying my tone, volume and pace to link specific content with stronger auditory associations. I would also read notes aloud as if I was *teaching* the content to a class or *explaining* a concept to someone who had never heard of it before.

This is a very effective technique. Convincing our brain that we not only need to recall content but that we must also be able to teach or explain it in a simple and clear way, forces us to remember it with greater clarity. In addition, if I found myself struggling to explain a concept, it often meant that I didn't understand it fully. I would then add it to my list of 'weaker topics' and set aside time in my plan to focus on it in more detail.

When reviewing notes, I would also have a scrap sheet of paper beside me where I would re-write the key words and concepts as I spoke them. I would not keep this scrap sheet of paper after finishing my review – the writing was often messy and unstructured. The purpose of making scrap notes was simply to reinforce the content being reviewed at that instant. I would repeat this process every time I reviewed my notes.

Occasionally, I would test myself using the *read-write-recite-repeat* technique. I would read through a section, re-write it on a scrap sheet of paper, and then cover *both* of them up with a plain sheet of paper. I would then recite the content I was trying to memorise until I was successful in doing so. This process could then be repeated until the notes were fully reviewed.

I was only able to follow this 'ideal' revision note-making process when I had a *good plan*. The time-consuming nature of hand-written notes meant that I had to set aside enough time to make detailed, dual-coded notes on all the topics.

And there were many occasions when I didn't have the time to do so...

In these scenarios, I would resort to *typing* revision notes on my laptop. I would quickly type notes in the *same* font and colour. This 'First Run-Through' would help me to re-familiarise myself with all the content of the course. I would then scroll to the top of the document and go through the notes again. On this 'Second Run-Through', I would add **bold** script, *italics*, underlines, different colours and other formatting changes to the notes. Re-reading the notes and selecting the appropriate words to format ensured that my mind was focused on the content of the words.

I would then print out the formatted revision notes. With a pen in hand, I would re-read them (aloud) and annotate them, drawing diagrams where relevant. Finally, as I approached the date of the exam, I would re-write my notes in a summarised form on scrap paper as I reviewed them.

This 'best of both worlds' approach was not ideal. However, it worked very effectively when I found myself with plenty to learn in a short space of time.

Notes - The Cure For Mental Recall Issues

Too many students that I've worked with have had a harmful habit of trying to *mentally* recall the content that they're trying to memorise. They don't recall it by speaking aloud. They don't recall it by writing it down. They simply try to recall a fact or answer in their mind...

...and then enter *panic mode* when they can't immediately recall it mentally!

This inability to recall an answer mentally can happen for many reasons. Most often, it's because we're *tired*. We tend to ask ourselves to mentally recall facts late in the day - or even worse, just before bed! When we find that we can't do it, we become stressed and anxious. Either we decide to 'panic study', only to become more stressed because we're not retaining any information, or we struggle to sleep because we feel unprepared, nervous and worried.

TOUGH GCSE WORKBOOK: SCIENCE | **REVISION TECHNIQUES**

One of my students, Nikki, first approached me because she had been experiencing a 'mental block' for several days. She felt that she hadn't retained anything that she'd been studying – and she was in the *middle* of her exams! The loss of confidence caused by this 'mental block' had rolled-over to her last two exams and caused her to panic when she saw a question for which she couldn't *immediately* remember the correct answer – even though after the exam, she realised that she actually *did* know how to do the question.

We tried to get to the root of the issue. In this case, the source turned out to be an unsuccessful attempt at mental recall six days earlier when Nikki was brushing her teeth before bed! She was exhausted and ready to sleep, had tried to recall a fact from her Biology A-Level paper – and had panicked when she couldn't immediately remember it!

Instead of simply checking her notes and reviewing the content, she suffered an anxiety attack!

I'm not telling you all of this to stress you out.

I'm telling you this because the solution is *so simple*.

TOUGH GCSE WORKBOOK: SCIENCE | **REVISION TECHNIQUES**

With the exception of oral examinations, you'll *never* have to mentally recall a fact, answer or solution in an exam! There will *always* be pen, paper and sufficient time for you to process the question, note down your thoughts, and recall the correct answer. Even if you don't recall the answer immediately, writing down a few key words can help to trigger your memory and aid you in remembering the answer.

And if you can't remember the answer during your revision, you can calmly get your textbook/notes, turn to the relevant page, and write down the correct answer. It's much easier to stay calm when you are processing facts externally (on a piece of paper) than trying to process them internally (in your own mind).

So, if you're going to practise mental recall during your revision, *write your thoughts and answers down,* and give yourself *time* to reach the answer. And most importantly, do *not* practise mental recall when you're tired!

Once we got to the root of the issue, Nikki was so relieved. Just confronting the source of the problem helped to alleviate the issue, as well as the knowledge that she always had a pen-and-paper during the exam to help her remember the content.

I'm grateful to share that the rest of her exams went *a lot* better! I'm also grateful to her for allowing me to share her story – she admitted that she was embarrassed about it, but that it would be worth it if it helped other students!

2. Past-Paper Mark-Scheme Tactics

A warning for this tool. It doesn't work for *everyone*. But we would suggest you try it for yourself, and see!

For subjects that are not assessed by essays (e.g. Maths, Sciences,), Past-Papers will often be accompanied by detailed Mark-Schemes. These will offer *worked solutions* for problems involving calculations, as well as *perfectly-worded written answers* for questions involving definitions or explanations.

In general, the *ideal* study process for Past-Papers involves completing the paper under exam conditions, checking our answers, and then using the Mark-Scheme to review what we did wrong. It's always worth setting aside time in our revision plans to complete a few Past-Papers (for example, those from the most recent years) in this manner.

However, when time is limited and there are *many* Past-Paper options available, it might not feasible to do every paper in this fashion.

When this was the case, print or download *both* the Past-Paper *and* the Mark-Scheme, and *copy* each Mark-Scheme answer out *by hand* on an A4 sheet of paper. This would be an *active, deliberate* process — there is no point during which you can copy out words without thinking about them. This should allow you to 'complete' each Past-Paper in *at least* half of the time that it would have taken to do so otherwise.

If you do this, don't just *read* the mark scheme. The benefit comes from *writing* down the answers in a conscious, thoughtful way. This helps to ingrain into our memories both the methods (for calculations) and the precise wording needed for full marks (for written answers) on the question.

This is not a *substitute* for doing Past-Papers properly — it's just an alternative to consider if you're constrained for time. It works best when you're confident about the content in your module, and are just trying to commit answers to memory and refine your exam technique.

In addition to this, try keeping a spreadsheet or a journal to *track* the questions that came up in Past-Papers. For each Past-Paper, write down a brief description of every question within it, and note down whether you found the question *easy, moderate* or *difficult*. This would help me to identify which topics you particularly struggled on, allowing you to specifically target those areas during my revision.

TOUGH GCSE WORKBOOK: SCIENCE — **REVISION TECHNIQUES**

With enough Past-Papers under your belt, you can also try to notice patterns to help with *predicting* some of the topics that might come up in your real exams. We must warn you that this is *not* accurate, and certainly not something to base your *entire* revision strategy on. If you decide to do this, use it to *supplement* your revision — not become the foundation for it. For example, if the same topic or question has come up in three of the last four past-papers, we don't lose much by spending a bit more time revising it. It may not come up — but if it does, we'll be prepared.

TOUGH GCSE WORKBOOK: SCIENCE | **REVISION TECHNIQUES**

We **strongly** recommend *against* 'tactically' ignoring topics altogether because you don't think they will come up in this year's exam based on Past-Paper trends. It just isn't worth feeling like an idiot during the exam when the topic *does* come up and you find yourself completely unprepared. Take it from us, we've been there, and you don't want to be explaining why you didn't revise a topic everyone else has looked at least once!

3. Pomodoro Technique

The Pomodoro Technique[8] is a simple productivity tool developed by Francisco Pomodoro in the 1980's. The idea is to work in *Pomodoros*. Each Pomodoro is a unit of time, lasting for 30 minutes, during which you *work* on your task for 25 minutes, and then take a *break* for five minutes. After four Pomodoros, you can take a longer break (15-30 minutes), before resetting the Pomodoro counter to 0. This technique has a number of advantages:

 Setting clear time boundaries reduces the impact of internal and external interruptions on study flow.

 Short, intense time intervals are very productive without being overly stressful – this is great if you've had a long day of work or school and can't face the thought of two hours of solid revision.

 We can convince ourselves to do anything for 'just 25 minutes' - including not checking our phones! Hour-long blocks can be daunting, and we'll often find reasons to procrastinate within them. A 25-minute burst of high productivity and no procrastination is manageable, even for those of us who are most easily distracted.

4. Metacognition

(Note: Metacognition means 'thinking about how we think' it's meta.)

In the context of studying for exams, it refers to the idea of strategising *how* we're going to study, instead of simply diving into the first task that we can think of.

Many of us tend to think less about *how* we're studying, and more on *how long* we're studying for. In doing so, we risk expending large amounts of time and effort doing work which doesn't actually translate to better performance in our exams.

By taking time to reflect on *how* we're going to approach our studies – for example, by considering the different study resources available to us and the different revision strategies we can implement – we increase the likelihood of performing better in our exams.

A 2017 study conducted at Stanford University showed that students who practised metacognition out-performed their peers on exams by the equivalent of one-third of a letter grade.[10] These students also reported feeling less stress and a greater sense of control over their performance than their peers.

How was metacognition practised in this study?

The selected students were first asked to consider the grade that they *wanted* to achieve, how *important* it was to them to achieve that grade, and how *likely* they thought they were to achieve it.

They were then asked to consider which types of *questions* the exam may include and the *study resources* they had available to them, such as lecture notes, practise questions, peer discussions, textbook readings and private tutoring. For each resource, they wrote down *why* that resource would be useful, and *how* they planned to utilise it in their exam preparation.

It's important to note that the selected students were chosen to ensure that there were no statistical differences in their performance compared to their peers prior to the exam. The students were also carefully chosen to ensure that there were no significant differences in their predicted grades, current motivation levels, and desired grades.[9]

So, what does all of this mean for you?

Before jumping into your studies, first think about *how* you are going to study. Be aware of the expectations and goals you have set for yourself. Recall some of your past exam performances and the key learning points you've taken away from them. Consider the study resources you have available to you and which would be most useful. Think about the exam itself and the types of questions you are likely to be asked. And then bring this information together to form a coherent study plan.

If you're still confused about whether you understand metacognition or not – by reading this book, you're already practising it!

Each activity and study tool outlined in this book is designed to make you *think* about how you currently study, whether a new tool or technique can help you to improve your studying process, and how you can implement it into your routine.

The reason that we have chosen to *explicitly* include metacognition as a studying technique is just to emphasise that scientific studies have *proved* that the steps involved in creating a study plan can help you to improve your exam performance.

5. Test-Based Learning

Self-testing has been shown to be more effective in increasing content retention compared with passive forms of studying, such as re-reading notes or re-watching lectures.[10] These 'tests' aren't like exams – they are simply ways for us to quiz ourselves on the content we're learning in a relaxed, low-stakes environment.

Creating flashcards to quiz yourself on, frequently practising past-paper questions, and doing Q&A sessions with study partners can all be effective ways of taking advantage of this.

6. Spaced Studying vs Night-Before Cramming

It might sound obvious, but studies have shown that spacing our studying is more effective than cramming when it comes to retaining information over a longer period of time.[11]

It's worth noting here that cramming can be slightly effective in the short-term for a one-off exam – however, as many of you might have experienced, you forget much of the information a week or month later. This is not helpful if you're being examined on similar content in the future.

If that wasn't bad enough, cramming also increases stress in the short-term and significantly decreases productivity *after* the exam – not ideal if you have another exam coming up within the next few days. Cramming is a consequence of poor planning and high anxiety. These can be removed altogether with a well-formed, long-term plan and an effective studying mindset. More information about how to set up and maintain these can be found in The Ultimate Exam Success Guide.

7. Interleaved Practice & Reviewing

Let's say that we have three modules to revise for: A, B and C. In this case, our plan is to spend three days on A, followed by three days on B, finishing with three days on C.

And after finishing C, we will realise that we have already forgotten most of the content from A...

Interleaving involves **mixing up** how we study these modules. In this case, we will study one day of A, followed by one day of B, followed by one day of C. We would then repeat this process until the modules were complete.

In other words, instead of AAABBBCCC, we'll study ABCABCABC.

In doing this, we're forcing our brain to recall the material covered in the past each time we revisit the module. This 'mini-review' strengthens the link between the content we covered previously and the content that we're covering now. It also signals to our brain that we need to be ready to recall information that may have been collected *more than one day ago*, increasing the likelihood of transferring the information from our *working memory* to our *long-term memory*.[12]

In addition, if you have two different exams in one day, we suggest you cover the first exam subject in the morning, and the second in the afternoon. This can help train your brain to begin associating the two subjects together so that you can recall material from both subjects with greater ease on Exam Day.

In general, working backwards from our exam dates is vital when creating a long-term plan that allows us to incorporate interleaved practice into our revision schedule.

8. Memory Devices (Mnemonics)

This technique is helpful for *memorising* content from our courses for our exams. There are three key principles behind the use of mnemonics.[13]

The first principle is **association**, which describes the way we connect the *thing* we're trying to remember to a *method* of remembering it (an *association image*). To recall what we're trying to remember, we then only need to recall the association image. Our minds work in different ways, so different associations will be more effective for each of us.

Examples of ways we can associate things include:

- Linking through colour, sound, shape or feeling.
- Merging, combining or wrapping things around each other.
- Imagining the objects crashing into or penetrating each other.
- Placing things on top of each other.

The second principle is **imagination**. Imagination is how we use our minds to create the links and associations that have the most meaning for us. The more strongly we can imagine or visualise an association, the more likely we are to remember it, so make them as creative, vivid, memorable – and even *weird* – as possible!

The final principle is **location**. Assigning a location to a particular mnemonic can strengthen our ability to remember it. Location provides us with a *context* for our information to further strengthen associations, and can also be used to *separate* unrelated mnemonics from each other.

TOUGH GCSE WORKBOOK: SCIENCE — **REVISION TECHNIQUES**

Our associations will be *unique* to each of us based on a combination of the way our mind works and the content that we're trying to memorise.

Nevertheless, here's a generic example which may clarify the principles of mnemonics:

Anthony is studying for his History GCSE exams. He is struggling because there are too many dates and events to remember. A particularly tough one for him was:

- The First Continental Congress took place in Philadelphia in September 1774, with Georgia being the only colony that chose not to send delegates.

He said that he had to be able to recall the year (1774) and the specific detail about Georgia for the exam. Any other details would be a bonus.

As mentioned, our minds work in different ways, so you might find the upcoming snapshot into my mind a bit surreal! You've been warned...

What he ended up doing was linking the number 74 to Georgia, and came up with an *association image* – a 74-year-old grandmother called Georgia!

He then added *imagination* – my 74-year old grandmother called Georgia was incredibly antisocial and would swear angrily at anyone who invited her to anything – *especially* the First Continental Congress! She was now loud, profane and incredibly animated.

Then Anthony added *location* – Philadelphia. The hometown of the cheese steak, the 76ers basketball team and the Fresh Prince of Bel-Air.

He can use these to reinforce the association – my antisocial 74-year old grandmother, Georgia, eating cheese steaks and angrily swearing at everyone around her. Once the association was firm, I returned to it and added details, for example that Grandma Georgia's birthday was in September.

Now you, too, can remember all about the First Continental Congress whenever you see Will Smith.

Experiment with mnemonics next time you are revising a content-heavy subject and discover what works best for you. Remember - the weirder, the better!

9. Commitment & Accountability

This very simple tool is effective for people who work better when they feel that they will be held *accountable* if they don't produce work within a defined period of time.

A study group is a great example of this. By committing to meet at a certain time to study, we feel an obligation to arrive on time, begin our tasks and continue working while in the presence of our study group.

However, study groups aren't always feasible. We might prefer to work alone, or other people may not be available. In this case, there are several actions we can take to create a sense of *accountability*.

For example, we can inform someone else of the tasks we need to complete on a given day, and *commit* to sending them *pictures* of each completed product (e.g. revision notes, past-paper questions) at specific times. We can also send a *time-lapse video* of ourselves studying for a period of time, or create a blog or social media account dedicated to studying where we upload photos of our work at regular times.

The combination of creating a *deadline* for our tasks alongside having people to hold us *accountable* drives us to complete our tasks quicker and with fewer distractions. The other person doesn't even *need* to do anything; just the *impression* of being held accountable if we miss the deadline can be sufficient as an incentive for us to commit to our tasks.

A cool sibling, cousin or parent is ideal for this role – we respect them enough to want to show them that we're working, but know that they won't get extensively involved and start to interrogate us on what we're doing and how much we're doing. The last thing we want is for (super-uncool) parents to start grilling us on why we only did 12 pages of revision notes instead of the 15 we 'promised' them!

10. Time-Lapse Videos

Here's an awesome trick from our buddy Kam again, which can be combined with the Commitment & Accountability technique above.

When I was in year 10, I decided to calculate my *productivity ratio* (yes, I know, how cool am I?) This is because I've always found it easier to convince myself to make improvements based on data I can actually *measure*. In this case, I wanted to identify how much of my 'time spent doing work' was *actually* spent doing work.

In other words, if I was working on a task for two hours, I wanted to figure out how much of that 2-hour period I spent *actually working* compared to the amount of time I spent staring out of the window, browsing TikTok, going to the fridge (etc.) while I considered myself to be working.

I decided to set up a time-lapse video on my iPhone to record myself over two hours, after which I would look through the footage and roughly calculate my productivity ratio. I connected my phone to a charger, loaded the time-lapse function, and got to work...

This experiment was an utter failure.

Why?
Because I worked steadily for *the entire 2 hours!*

Psychologically speaking, I couldn't bear to find out my *true* unproductivity levels. I didn't want to accept any tangible evidence that *proved* that I was inefficient and easily distracted. So, knowing that I was recording myself, I convinced myself to *stay seated* and *continue working* each time I felt the temptation to get up from my desk.

As a result, I managed to do *productive work* for longer than ever before without taking a break!

So, the experiment failed – I didn't figure out a realistic value for my productive work ratio. But in failing, I learned a powerful productivity trick: *we always do more when we're being filmed!*

Set up your time-lapses for about 40-60 minutes and see how it works for you. Even if you don't feel more productive, you'll be able to figure out a realistic representation of your productivity ratio (which you can then focus on improving). And at the very worst, you simply won't be distracted by your phone while studying – it's hard to check messages when there's a time-lapse recording and your phone is out of reach!

> **Activity 2.3:** Of the 10 studying techniques described above, which ones would you like to integrate into your studying process? How can you begin implementing them?

The more we practise applying these techniques, the *easier* they become to apply, and the *better* we become at using them. Once you've decided on the techniques you want to experiment with, use your plan to help you get into a *habit* of applying them. Applying these techniques often (*frequency*) at regular times (*regularity*) for specific tasks (*specificity*) is the key to creating *habits*.

So far, we've discussed key insights from the Learning Styles model, whether you're a time or task-focused worker, and ten useful study techniques to help you achieve Exam Success.

Enough of the '*how*' – time to move on to the '*where*' and '*when*'.

TOUGH GCSE WORKBOOK: SCIENCE | **IDEAL REVISION SPACE**

Where You Study: Creating The Perfect Study Environment

Our optimal study environment is different for each of us. In identifying yours, there are several factors to take into account.

Social or Solitary Preferences

The first of these is identifying whether you're a social or solitary learner.

Social learners might choose locations where they are not only surrounded by other people but can also communicate freely with study partners. Nonetheless, if studying in groups, they should be diligent in ensuring that they limit their communication to studying topics. Try to allocate a defined period of time to cover notes individually, followed by time to discuss or quiz each other on the content covered, followed by a few minutes of relaxed chatting.

Ideas of locations for social learners and their study partners or groups include:

- Classrooms or meeting rooms.
- Coffee shops or other public areas.
- Living room or kitchen.

Solitary learners are often quite sensitive about their environment, and as such prefer to study where they feel most *comfortable*. This largely depends on individual preferences. In general, their study locations are selected to minimise interactions with other people and prevent them from being interrupted during studying.

Ideas of locations for solitary learners include:

TOUGH GCSE WORKBOOK: SCIENCE — IDEAL REVISION SPACE

 Libraries

 Bedroom (or other room where you won't be interrupted)

If you are a solitary learner though, you may dislike working in classrooms and *can't stand* the dreary atmosphere in libraries. Working in a home/ dormitory environment where is absolutely fine, though if it is *possible* we recommend you physically separate my work-area from my sleep-area. This means try to avoid working in your bedroom if you can. If that is the only quiet spot you can find, we suggest at least that you try not to work in bed, work at a desk or, if you don't have one, on a chair or the floor.

The Perfect Personal Workspace

It can be useful to create a personal workspace where we can completely focus our attention on studying. Our workspace should be a well-lit location with minimal distractions. It should be kept tidy and organised, as any clutter creates a *visual* distraction that makes it easier for our *mind* to become distracted by external stimuli.

We must *leave* our personal workspace during our breaks. This helps us to create a mental association between sitting at our workspace and *only* doing productive studying. Creating this physical separation between 'where we work' and 'where we don't work' also allows us to mentally *detach* from our work, which is vital to our mental health and well-being.

Make it a *habit* to sit at your workspace and immediately begin studying, and to leave it as soon as you finish. Remember – *motivation* is what gets us started when we begin a new routine, but *habit* is what keeps us going even when our motivation falters! If you create a habit to sit there at specific times and *immediately* begin work, you don't give your mind the option to create negative thoughts about whether you want to study, how much you have left to do, and other thoughts that may keep us stuck in the Pit of Eternal Procrastination.

Before we begin studying, we should prepare our workspace with all our stationery, necessary textbooks and a glass or bottle of water.

Activity 2.4: Create your own personal workspace. Where will it be? What will you choose to have in your space? What can you do to make a habit of only doing productive work at your workspace?

Music & Background Noise
There has been no *unanimous* scientific evidence on the impact of music on studying. The best course of action is simply to *experiment* and discover what works best for you.

That being said, silence (an absence of music) has been consistently linked to *better* performance and memory retention in tasks compared to when different types of music were present.[4] However, it must be taken into account that the sample sizes for the studies were very small, so results may not be representative.

TOUGH GCSE WORKBOOK: SCIENCE   **IDEAL REVISION SPACE**

For those who insist on listening to music while studying, it's important to remember that listening to music while doing repetitive homework or coursework tasks is significantly *different* from listening to music when we're revising.

During homework or coursework, many of us listen to music as it helps to relieve the 'boredom' we associate with repetitive tasks. In many cases, music even *stops* us from getting distracted by whatever is going on in our immediate environment. Many of us find that we can 'zone-in' with our headphones on, as if they create a *barrier* that prevents our mind from being distracted by our surroundings, and even our own thoughts.

However, revising for exams or learning new content is *very* different. The purpose of revision is to focus on getting our brain to *remember* or *understand* a process or fact which has not been committed to memory beforehand. Listening to music distracts the brain from the content we're trying to revise, and makes it harder for our brain to process the information and commit it to memory.

If you *still* insist on listening to music while you revise, it may be worth considering that listening to instrumental music in the background at a low volume may be a better alternative to music that contains *lyrics*, especially at higher volumes. Listening to music with lyrics can be compared to having someone talking in the background – except that you might be tempted to want to *join in* with the conversation! We particularly recommend things like video game soundtracks, if you need music to study effectively, as they very rarely contain any words, and are *designed* to fade into the background while you blast space invaders (or whatever it is the cool kids are playing these days).

TOUGH GCSE WORKBOOK: SCIENCE | **IDEAL REVISION SPACE**

If you find it difficult to work in silence, it may also be worth considering ambient background music with few instruments and little variation throughout, or natural sounds like falling rain or birds chirping. Another option is to *read your content out loud*, whether it's directly from a textbook or as you're writing notes. On an interesting note, some people might find that they can quite easily create memory associations between the content they are revising and a song playing in the background.

We actually tried this one ourselves and while we can admit that it does work... it may also ruin the song forever!

However, listening to music during a 5-minute Pomodoro breaks can be a great way to refresh your mind for the studying ahead. Will this work for you? Try it and find out. As mentioned at the start, the effect that music has on your studies *depends on you as an individual*.

> **Activity 2.5:** Reflect on how you use music when studying. Is the music you are listening to helping or hindering your studying? What can you change in order to improve your situation?

Minimising External Distractions

Distractions are everywhere. Here are five of the most common sources, as well as actions we can take to prevent them from becoming distractions:

1. **Phones/ Tablets (texts, social media, apps etc.)**
   - Store them away from your workspace, put them on 'flight mode', or turn them off completely.
   - Allocate set time periods to address text messages or social media (for example, during 5-minute breaks of Pomodoros) – but be disciplined!

2. **Laptops/ Computers (social media, You-Tube, Reddit etc.)**
   - Shut down/ sleep mode if they are not needed for study purposes.
   - Close distracting tabs as soon as you are finished with them.
   - Allocate set time periods for recreational Internet use.
   - Set up search engine add-ons which prevent you from accessing specific websites at certain times.

3. **Television/ Netflix**
    - Allocate set time periods for watching TV/Netflix shows.
    - Avoid revising with the TV on in the background.
    - Do NOT start a new TV series close to exams! Seriously. Just don't.

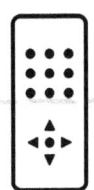

4. **People (family, friends, partner, colleagues)**
    - Inform family and friends of your study timetable so that you don't get disturbed – they'll be happy to support you in your efforts.
    - Set aside time for fun activities with friends, ensuring that your *priority tasks* (<u>Principle 1</u>) are being fulfilled first.

5. **Physical Needs (hunger, thirst, motion, sleep)**
    - These ones are hopefully pretty obvious, and super important.

However, just because we've done our best to anticipate these distractions, they may still crop up occasionally.

As such, we also need to understand *when* we become most susceptible to distractions. We'll discuss four very common examples below:

TOUGH GCSE WORKBOOK: SCIENCE   **IDEAL REVISION SPACE**

1. Tired or *fatigued*

When we become **mentally fatigued**, our studying becomes unproductive. Our frustration and dissatisfaction increases, and we become easily distracted. Once distracted, it also becomes harder to return our attention to our work.

- If your fatigue stems from low energy, consider taking a brisk walk outdoors or doing some exercise. Ensure that you are drinking healthy amounts of water and avoid foods that cause energy to 'spike' and 'drop'.

- If your fatigue stems from tiredness, your productivity will only continue to decrease. Consider taking a nap, or even going to bed early.

- If your fatigue stems from low motivation, grab a pen and paper and explore *why* your motivation is low, and focus on what you can do to increase it *now*.

- If your fatigue stems from stress or anxiety, consider doing exercise, taking a walk outdoors, listening to music, doing some mindfulness practices, and generally doing relaxing activities.

2. Not enjoying or *bored* by the content that we're studying
If we find ourselves distracted because we're **not enjoying the process of studying**, we need to remind ourselves of the *purpose* of our study process and the goals that we're trying to achieve.

The most simple and effective way of doing this is to grab a pen and sheet of paper and *write down* the goal that we're trying to achieve through our studying.

The physical action of writing not only breaks the mental aspect of distraction, but by *writing* our goals down again, we realign with our reason for *why* we're studying.

3. Offered a *more desirable alternative* (MDA) to studying
A **more desirable alternative (MDA)** to studying can mean anything from seeing friends or going out for dinner, to participating in leisure activities or watching Netflix. We have to be aware of the consequences that giving in to these temptations may have on our studies.

In some cases, we may check our plans and find that we can easily adapt our schedule. We can then make a choice to take up the offer of the MDA. Studying doesn't *have* to be an arduous, boring process, and this is exactly what planning allows us to do – study effectively, but also participate in the activities that we enjoy completely guilt-free.

However, in other cases, we become distracted by MDAs in a bid to *escape* from our study commitments, despite the setbacks we know it may cause.

Many of us start studying, but constantly stop and check our phone for MDAs. Replying to a message, a quick walk to Tescos with a friend, a coffee break with her sister — any of them were *more desirable* than studying.

But many of us would also feel *guilty* about this. In time, we become unable to *fully enjoy* any of the activities we are doing because we know we should be studying.

The solution is to do your studies first, and then enjoy your MDAs guilt-free!

This is something that most of us recognise when we're reminded of it. However, by bringing it to our awareness and having it at the forefront of our mind, we can use that reasoning to avoid the temptation of MDAs.

4. In the *gap* between finishing one task and beginning another

The **gap between finishing one task and starting another** can be our best friend or our worst enemy.

At best, in can be a short, relaxing break; an opportunity to refresh our minds, replenish our hunger for knowledge, and recover our focus to attack the task at hand.

At worst, it can set off a crazy cycle of procrastination...

One YouTube video becomes thirty; messaging a friend on Snap turns into a memefest for the next hour; replying to a text becomes trawling through Instagram while we wait for our friend to reply...

By becoming aware of how we use the *gap between tasks*, we can set ourselves boundaries to ensure that we stay within the '*optimal rest time*' category, instead of entering a crazy cycle of procrastination.

Set firm time intervals or reminders to return to work. Avoid texting or social media activities until later in the day when you feel comfortable with the study progress you have made. Realign with your goals by reminding yourself of *why* studying will help you achieve what you want.

> **Activity 2.6: Write down your main sources of distraction. How can you manage them more effectively? How can you set measures in place to stop yourself from becoming easily distracted?**

Now that we have a better understanding of our optimal study environment and how we can minimise the distractions within it, we can consider *when* we study.

When You Study: Finding The Perfect Study Time

In the debate between 'daytime' and 'night-time' studying, scientific research is yet to provide any evidence for an objective 'best time' to study. It comes down to individual preference and an awareness of the advantages and disadvantages of each.

The majority of us are familiar with **daytime studying**. Most schools run courses and lessons during the morning and afternoon (can you imagine going to a school which only ran at night?? Would make hide-and-seek way more interesting... you still play hide-and-seek right? Right!?) We study in the evening and sleep at night in anticipation of the next day's lessons. Keeping to this structure has various advantages:

1. Society is structured in such a way that we're active by day and asleep by night. Libraries, coffee shops and other public locations are often only open during the day. Lessons are also mostly run during the day. In the event of needing help, teachers, friends and colleagues may also only be available during daytime hours.

2. As human beings, we respond to natural light differently to artificial light. Artificial light is worse for our eyesight. It can also disturb our biological body clock and natural circadian rhythms, causing detrimental shifts in our sleep patterns.

3. Exams are often carried out during the morning or early afternoon. Daytime study prepares our mind to be working at its optimum *during* the time we'll have our exams.

TOUGH GCSE WORKBOOK: SCIENCE   **STUDY TIME**

Night-time studying has become increasingly popular, although many more factors need to be considered in implementing it successfully. It's impossible to pull off during term time, and is not something we really recommend even in the holidays. It's important to establish a consistent routine to ensure that our body adapts to night-time study, instead of fluctuating back and forth between night-time and daytime study, which creates a feeling akin to bad jet-lag.

Maintaining a well-lit room is important to night-time studying, both in terms of keeping our mind alert and preventing excessive straining of our eyes. It's also easier to lose track of time at night, making it vital to manage and track our time effectively. Setting a timer to drink water regularly is also recommended. We should ensure that we have a supply of good-quality food, since supermarkets and coffee shops are likely to be shut.

In terms of sleeping patterns, some people prefer to nap more frequently during the day to account for less sleep each night. Others shift their sleeping habits entirely, sleeping anytime between 2PM and 6PM in order to wake up between 10PM and 2AM!

Night-time study does have some advantages:

1. The 'feeling of peace and quiet' is one of the most prominent advantages of night-time study. The decreased intensity and activity around you can create a more relaxed atmosphere in which to study.
2. There are fewer distractions – people are sleeping, and there are no lessons to attend or activities to join. It becomes

easier to lose yourself in a work 'flow' when interruptions around you are at a minimum, which can translate to more effective studying.

3. Many people find that their creativeness increases at night-time. Concepts and problems may be looked at from different perspectives, some of which might be more conducive to remembering or understanding content.

To conclude, there is no *right* time to study. As individuals, we need to assess what works best for us, and always keep in mind the time which we're going to be sitting each exam. Do bear in mind, though, that studying during term time kinda has to be on a day cycle!!!

> **Activity 2.7:** Reflect on your most productive study times during the day. Are these optimal to ensure that you are awake and focused when sitting your exams? If not, what can you do to change this?

In summary:
- We have discussed the importance of *how* we study and looked at different techniques we can use to prepare more effectively for our exams.
- We have analysed the impact of *where* we study in the context of our personality, work environment and susceptibility to distractions.
- We have considered the advantages of *when* we study in the context of day-time and night-time studying.

With a better understanding of how we study, where we study and when we study, we can better focus on how to do the best revision possible for us – and make the most of our GCSE science revision, and our practice questions.

For more hints and tips for great revision – check out the Ultimate Guide to Exam Success.

Tough GCSE Science Questions:

There is always scope in your GCSE exams for the examiners to ask questions which are more complicated or challenging than the vast majority of others. Occasionally, this can be due to an error of judgment on the part of the examiners, but this isn't true most of the time, generally, they just want to stretch you, and see what the very best GCSE students are capable of. This is especially true for Science GCSEs.

Increasingly in schools in the UK, teachers are doing their best to teach students in challenging circumstances, and this can mean that your GCSE preparation is limited to the bare minimum of what the specification requires. It's important then that, in the run up to those crucial exams, you have gone the extra mile to make sure that you have done the preparation that your teachers want to do, but don't have time for.

In the rest of this book, we are going to provide hundreds of practice questions for biology, chemistry and physics, all of which are designed to test the very best GCSE candidates. You should find them challenging, but not impossible. You will want to be sure that you know your specifications well before your exam, and this book can be a very useful tool for that. If you regularly find that you are getting less than half of the questions right, then there's a good chance that there are gaps in your knowledge and techniques which you need to fill.

In the case of biology, the majority of the questions you will be asked will rely primarily on memory recall - there is a lot of information you have to memorise for the GCSE, and they want to see how well you've done so.

In general, you want to ensure that you are familiar with the following topics (regardless of which exam board you are using, in order to give you the best change of answering the full range of potential difficult questions that you could face similar ones to in your exams:

- Structure of animal, plant and bacterial cells
- Osmosis, Diffusion and Active Transport
- Cell Division (mitosis + meiosis)
- Family pedigrees and Inheritance
- DNA structure and replication
- Gene Technology & Stem Cells
- Enzymes – Function, mechanism and examples of digestive enzymes
- Aerobic and Anaerobic Respiration
- The central vs. peripheral nervous system
- The respiratory cycle including movement of ribs and diaphragm
- The Cardiac Cycle
- Hormones

- Basic immunology
- Food chains and food webs
- The carbon and nitrogen cycles

For chemistry and physics, there are plenty of things that you will need to remember, of course, but there is also a greater focus on mathematical skill and information processing abilities, you need to be good at maths, and working out the solutions to complex problems in a very short space of time, and with little or no reference material outside of your own brain.

For chemistry, there are certain particular skills that it is important that you practice, such as balancing equations and mass calculations, because they tend to be the focus of a lot of tough GCSE science questions, and catch out a lot of students. We have a couple of tips for those here, which might explain things in a different way to how you've looked at them before, we hope they'll be useful for those of you struggling with that material!

Balancing Equations

For some reason, most students are rarely shown how to formally balance equations – including those studying it at GCSE. Balancing equations intuitively or via trial and error will only get you so far in your GCSEs as the equations you'll have to work with will be fairly complex. To avoid wasting valuable time, it is essential you learn a method that will allow you to solve these in less than 60 seconds on a consistent basis. The method shown below is the simplest way and requires you to be able to do quick mental arithmetic (which is something you should be aiming for anyway). The following equation shows the reaction between Iodic acid, hydrochloric acid and copper Iodide:

$$a\ HIO_3 + b\ CuI_2 + c\ HCl \rightarrow d\ CuCl_3 + e\ ICl + f\ H_2O$$

What values of **a, b, c, d, e** and **f** are needed in order to balance the equation?

	a	b	c	d	e	f
A	5	4	25	4	13	15
B	5	4	20	4	8	15
C	5	6	20	6	8	15
D	2	8	10	8	8	15
E	6	8	24	10	16	15
F	6	10	22	10	16	15

Step 1: Pick an element and see how many atoms there are on the left and right sides.

Step 2: Form an equation to represent this. For Cu: b = d

Step 3: See if any of the answer options don't satisfy b=d. In this case, for option E, b is 8 and d is 10. This allows us to eliminate option E.

Once you've eliminated as many options as possible, go back to step 1 and pick another element.

For Hydrogen (H): a + c = 2. Then see if any of the answer options don't satisfy a + c = 2f.

- Option A: 5 + 25 is equal to 2 × 15
- Option B: 5 + 20 is not equal to 2 × 15
- Option C: 5 + 20 is not equal to 2 × 15
- Option D: 2 + 10 is not equal to 2 × 15

This allows us to eliminate option B, C and D. E has already been eliminated. Thus, the only solution possible is A. This method works best when you get given a table above as this allows you to quickly eliminate options. However, it is still a viable method even if you don't get this information.

CHEMISTRY CALCULATIONS

Equations you **MUST** know:
- Atomic Mass = Mass/Moles
- Amount (mol) = Concentration (mol/dm^3) x Volume (dm^3)

Avogadro's Constant:
One mole of anything contains 6×10^{23} of it e.g. 5 Moles of water contain $5 \times 6 \times 10^{23}$ number of water molecules.

Abundances:
The average atomic mass takes the abundances of all isotopes into account. Thus:
A_r = (Abundance of Isotope 1) x (Mass of Isotope 1) + (Abundance of Isotope 2) x (Mass of Isotope 2) +...

As for physics, you must make sure that you are confident with commonly examined topics like Newtonian mechanics, electrical circuits, and radioactive decay.

The first step to improving in this section is to memorise by rote all the equations listed on the next page.
The majority of the physics questions involve a fair bit of maths – this means you need to be comfortable with converting between units and also powers of 10. **Most questions require two step calculations**. Consider the example:

A metal ball is released from the roof a 20 metre building. Assuming air resistance equals is negligible; calculate the velocity at which the ball hits the ground. [g = 10ms^{-2}]

A. 5 ms^{-1} C. 15 ms^{-1} E. 25 ms^{-1}
B. 10 ms^{-1} D. 20 ms^{-1}

When the ball hits the ground, all of its gravitational potential energy has been converted to kinetic energy. Thus, $E_p = E_k$:

$mg\Delta h = \frac{mv^2}{2}$

Thus, $v = \sqrt{2gh} = \sqrt{2 \times 10 \times 20}$
$= \sqrt{400} = 20 ms^{-1}$

Here, you were required to not only recall two equations but apply and rearrange them very quickly to get the answer; all in under 60 seconds. Thus, it is easy to understand why the physics questions are generally much harder than the biology and chemistry ones.

Note that if you were comfortable with basic Newtonian mechanics, you could have also solved this using a single suvat equation: $v^2 = u^2 + 2as$

$v = \sqrt{2 \times 10 \times 20} = 20 ms^{-1}$

This is why you're **strongly advised to learn the 'suvat' equations** on the next page even if they're technically not on the syllabus.

SI UNITS

Remember that in order to get the correct answer you must always work in SI units i.e. do your calculations in terms of metres (not centimetres) and kilograms (not grams), etc.

> *Top tip!* Knowing SI units is extremely useful because they allow you to **'work out' equations** if you ever forget them e.g. The units for density are kg/m^3. Since Kg is the SI unit for mass, and m^3 is represented by volume – the equation for density must be = Mass/Volume.

Formulas you MUST know:

Equations of Motion:
- $s = ut + 0.5at^2$
- $v = u + at$
- $a = (v-u)/t$
- $v^2 = u^2 + 2as$

Equations relating to Force:
- Force = mass × acceleration
- Force = Momentum/Time
- Pressure = Force / Area

- Moment of a Force = Force x Distance
- Work done = Force x Displacement

For objects in equilibrium:
- Sum of Clockwise moments = Sum of Anti-clockwise moments
- Sum of all resultant forces = 0

Equations relating to Energy:
- Kinetic Energy = $0.5 mv^2$
- Δ in Gravitational Potential Energy = $mg\Delta h$
- Energy Efficiency = (Useful energy/ Total energy) x 100%

Equations relating to Power:
- Power = Work done / time
- Power = Energy transferred / time
- Power = Force x velocity

Electrical Equations:
- $Q = It$
- $V = IR$
- $P = IV = I^2 R = V^2/R$
- V = Potential difference (V, Volts)
- R = Resistance (Ohms)
- P = Power (W, Watts)
- Q = Charge (C, Coulombs)
- t = Time (s, seconds)

For Transformers: $\frac{V_p}{V_s} = \frac{n_p}{n_s}$ where:

- V: Potential difference
- n: Number of turns
- p: Primary
- s: Secondary

Other:
- Weight = mass × g
- Density = Mass / Volume
- Momentum = Mass × Velocity
- g = 9.81 ms-2 (unless otherwise stated)

Factor	Text	Symbol
10^{12}	Tera	T
10^{9}	Giga	G
10^{6}	Mega	M
10^{3}	Kilo	k
10^{2}	Hecto	h
10^{-1}	Deci	d
10^{-2}	Centi	c
10^{-3}	Milli	m
10^{-6}	Micro	μ
10^{-9}	Nano	n
10^{-12}	Pico	p

TOUGH GCSE WORKBOOK: SCIENCE — STUDY TIME

With no further ado, you can work through the practice questions below. Whenever you come across an area of weakness, or gap in your knowledge, take time to revise those topics before carrying on. There's little point at trying these questions, or aiming for top level marks in your Science GCSEs with gaps in what you can do!

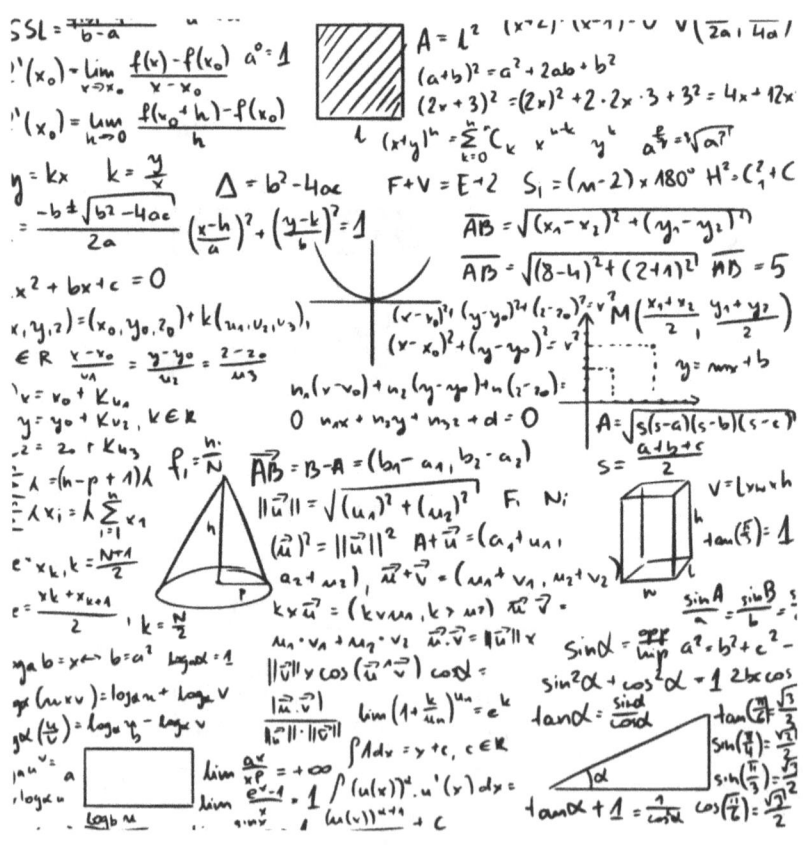

BIOLOGY QUESTIONS

Question 1:
In relation to the human genome, which of the following statements are correct?

1. The genome is encoded by 4 different bases in DNA.
2. The sugar backbone of the DNA strand is formed of glucose.
3. DNA is found in the nucleus of bacteria.

A. 1 only
B. 2 only
C. 3 only
D. 1 and 2
E. 1 and 3

Question 2:
Animal cells contain organelles that take part in vital metabolic processes. Which of the following is true?

1. The majority of energy production by animal cells occurs in the mitochondria.
2. The cell wall protects the animal cell membrane from outside pressure differences.
3. Chloroplasts are not present in animal cells.

A. 1 only
B. 2 only
C. 3 only
D. 1 and 3
E. 2 and 3

Question 3:
With regards to animal mitochondria, which of the following is correct?

A. Mitochondria are not necessary for aerobic respiration.
B. Mitochondria are enveloped by a double membrane.
C. Mitochondria are more abundant in skeletal muscle than fat cells.
D. The majority of DNA replication happens inside mitochondria.
E. The majority of protein synthesis occurs in mitochondria.

Question 4:
In relation to bacteria, which of the following is FALSE?

A. Bacteria always lead to disease.
B. Bacteria contain plasmid DNA.
C. Bacteria do not contain mitochondria.
D. Bacteria have a cell wall and a plasma membrane.
E. Some bacteria are susceptible to antibiotics.

Question 5:
In relation to bacterial replication, which of the following is correct?

A. Bacteria undergo sexual reproduction.
B. Bacteria have a nucleus.
C. Bacteria carry genetic information on circular plasmids.
D. Bacterial genomes are formed of RNA instead of DNA.
E. Bacteria require gametes to replicate.

Question 6
Which of the following statements are correct regarding active transport?

A. ATP is necessary and sufficient for active transport.
B. ATP is not necessary but is sufficient for active transport.
C. The relative concentrations of the material being transported have little impact on the rate of active transport.
D. Transport proteins are necessary and sufficient for active transport.
E. Active transport relies on transport proteins that are powered by an electrochemical gradient.

Question 7:
Concerning mammalian reproduction, which of the following is FALSE?

A. Fertilisation involves the fusion of two gametes.
B. Reproduction is sexual and the offspring display genetic variation.
C. Reproduction relies upon the exchange of genetic material.
D. Mammalian gametes are diploid cells produced via meiosis.
E. Embryonic growth requires carefully controlled mitosis.

Question 8:
Which of the following apply to Mendelian inheritance?

1. It only applies to plants.
2. It treats different traits as either dominant or recessive.
3. Heterozygotes have a 25% chance of expressing a recessive trait.

A. 1 only
B. 2 only
C. 3 only
D. 1 and 2
E. 1 and 3

Question 9:
Which of the following statements are correct?

A. Hormones are secreted into the blood stream and act over long distances at specific target organs.
B. Hormones are substances that almost always cause muscles to contract.
C. Hormones have no impact on the nervous or enteric systems.
D. Hormones are always derived from food and never synthesised.
E. Hormones act rapidly to restore homeostasis.

Question 10:
With regard to neuronal signalling in the body, which of the following are true?

1. Neuronal transmission can be caused by both electrical and chemical stimulation.
2. Synapses ultimately result in the production of an electrical current for signal transduction.
3. All synapses in humans are electrical and unidirectional.

A. 1 only
B. 2 only
C. 3 only
D. 1 and 2
E. 1 and 3

Question 11:
What is the primary reason that pH is controlled so tightly in the human body?

A. To allow rapid protein synthesis.
B. To allow for effective digestion throughout the GI tract.
C. To ensure ions can function properly in neural signalling.
D. To ensure enzymes are able to function properly.
E. To prevent changes in core body temperature.

Question 12:
Which of the following statements are correct regarding the bacterial cell wall?

1. It confers bacteria protection against external environmental stimuli.
2. It is an evolutionary remnant and now has little functional significance in most bacteria.
3. It is made up primarily of glucose in bacteria.

A. Only 1
B. Only 2
C. Only 3
D. 1 and 2
E. 2 and 3

Question 13:
Which of the following statements are correct regarding mitosis?

1. It is important in sexual reproduction.
2. A single round of mitosis results in the formation of 2 genetically distinct daughter cells.
3. Mitosis is vital for tissue growth, as it is the basis for cell multiplication.

A. Only 1
B. Only 2
C. Only 3
D. 1 and 2
E. 2 and 3

Question 14:
Which of the following is the best definition of a mutation?

A. A mutation is a permanent change in DNA.
B. A mutation is a permanent change in DNA that is harmful to an organism.
C. A mutation is a permanent change in the structure of intra-cellular organelles caused by changes in DNA/RNA.
D. A mutation is a permanent change in chromosomal structure caused by DNA/RNA changes.

Question 15:
In relation to mutations, which of the following statements are correct?

1. Mutations always lead to discernible changes in the phenotype of an organism.
2. Mutations are central to natural processes such as evolution.
3. Mutations play a role in cancer.

A. Only 1
B. Only 2
C. Only 3
D. 1 and 2
E. 2 and 3

Question 16:
Which of the following is the most accurate definition of an antibody?

A. An antibody is a molecule that protects red blood cells from changes in pH.
B. An antibody is a molecule produced only by humans and has a pivotal role in the immune system.
C. An antibody is a toxin produced by a pathogen to damage the host organism.
D. An antibody is a molecule that is used by the immune system to identify and neutralize foreign objects and molecules.
E. Antibodies are small proteins found in red blood cells that help increase oxygen carriage.

Question 17:
Which of the following statements about the kidney are correct?

1. The kidneys filter the blood and remove waste products from the body.
2. The kidneys are involved in the digestion of food.
3. In a healthy individual, the kidneys produce urine that contains high levels of glucose.

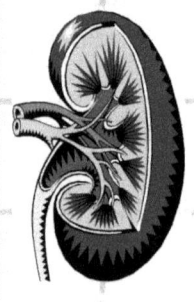

A. Only 1
B. Only 2
C. Only 3
D. 1 and 2
E. 2 and 3

Question 18:
Which of the following statements are correct?

1. Hormones are slower acting than nerves.
2. Hormones act for a very short time.
3. Hormones act more generally than nerves.
4. Hormones are released when you are frightened.

A. 1 only
B. 1 and 3 only
C. 2 and 4 only
D. 1, 3 and 4 only
E. 1, 2, 3 and 4

Question 19:
Which statements about homeostasis are correct?
1. Homeostasis is about ensuring the inputs within your body exceed the outputs to maintain a constant internal environment.
2. Homeostasis is about ensuring the inputs within your body are less than the outputs to maintain a constant internal environment.
3. Homeostasis is about balancing the inputs and outputs within your body to make it fluctuate with the environment.
4. Homeostasis is about balancing the inputs within your body with the outputs to maintain a constant internal environment.

A. 1 only
B. 2 only
C. 3 only
D. 4 only
E. 1 and 3 only

Question 20:
Which of the following statements regarding the food chain is true?

A. There is more energy and biomass each time you move up a trophic level.
B. There is less energy and biomass each time you move up a trophic level.
C. There is more energy but less biomass each time you move up a trophic level.
D. There is less energy but more biomass each time you move up a trophic level.
E. There is no difference in the energy or biomass when you move up a trophic level.

Question 21:
Which of the following statements are true about asexual reproduction?

1. There is no fusion of gametes.
2. There are two parents.
3. There is no mixing of chromosomes.
4. Binary fission is an example of asexual reproduction.

A. 1, 3 and 4 only
B. 1 and 3 only
C. 1 and 4 only
D. 3 and 4 only
E. All are true

TOUGH GCSE WORKBOOK: SCIENCE

BIOLOGY QUESTIONS

Question 22:
Put the following components of a stimulus-response arc in the order in which they are activated when Jonas sees a bowl of chicken and moves towards it.

1. Retina
2. Motor neuron
3. Sensory neuron
4. Brain
5. Muscle

A. 1 - 3 - 4 - 5 - 2
B. 1 - 2 - 3 - 4 - 5
C. 5 - 1 - 3 - 2 - 4
D. 1 - 3 - 2 - 4 - 5
E. 1 - 3 - 4 - 2 - 5

Question 23:
The following statements relate to the flow of blood through the heart.

1. The right-hand side of the heart contains deoxygenated blood.
2. The aorta receives oxygenated blood from the left atrium.
3. The heart pumps deoxygenated blood into the pulmonary vein.
4. Valves are present to prevent flow of blood from the left ventricle to the right ventricle.

Which of these statements is / are correct?

A. 3 only
B. 1 and 3
C. 2 and 4
D. 1 only
E. None of the above

TOUGH GCSE WORKBOOK: SCIENCE — BIOLOGY QUESTIONS

Question 24:
Which of the following statements are true about animal cloning?

1. Animals cloned from embryo transplants are genetically identical.
2. The genetic material is removed from an unfertilised egg during adult cell cloning.
3. Cloning can cause a reduced gene pool.
4. Cloning is only possible with mammals.

A. 1 only
B. 2 only
C. 1 and 2 only
D. 4 only
E. 1, 2 and 3 only

Question 25:
Which of the following statements are true with regards to evolution?

1. Individuals within a species show variation because of differences in their genes.
2. Beneficial mutations will accumulate within a population.
3. Gene differences are caused by sexual reproduction and mutations.
4. Species with similar characteristics never have similar genes.

A. 1 only
B. 1 and 4 only
C. 2 and 3 only
D. 2 and 4 only
E. 1, 2 and 3 only

Question 26:
Which of the following statements about genetics are correct?

1. Alleles are a similar version of different cells.
2. If you are homozygous for a trait, you have three alleles the same for that particular gene.
3. If you are heterozygous for a trait, you have two different alleles for that particular gene.
4. To show the characteristic that is caused by a recessive allele, both carried alleles for the gene have to be recessive.

A. 1 only
B. 2 only
C. 3 only
D. 4 only
E. 3 and 4 only

Question 27:
Which of the following statements are correct about meiosis?

1. The DNA content of a gamete is half that of a human red blood cell.
2. Meiosis requires ATP.
3. Meiosis only takes place in reproductive tissue.
4. In meiosis, a diploid cell divides in such a way so as to produce two haploid cells.

A. 1 only
B. 3 only
C. 1 and 2 only
D. 2 and 3 only
E. 2 and 4 only

Question 28:
Put the following statements in the correct order of events for when there is too little water in the blood.

1. Urine is more concentrated
2. Pituitary gland releases ADH
3. Blood water level returns to normal
4. Hypothalamus detects too little water in blood
5. Kidney affects water level

A. 1 - 2 - 3 - 4 - 5   C. 4 - 2 - 5 - 1 - 3   E. 5 - 2 - 3 - 4 - 1
B. 5 - 4 - 3 - 2 - 1   D. 3 - 2 - 4 - 1 - 5

Question 29:
The pH of venous blood is 7.35. Which of the following is the likely pH of arterial blood?

A. 5.2   C. 7.0   E. 8.0
B. 6.5   D. 7.4

Question 30:
Which of the following statements are true of the cytoplasm?

1. The vast majority of the cytoplasm is made up of water.
2. All contents of animal cells are contained in the cytoplasm.
3. The cytoplasm contains electrolytes and proteins.

A. 1 only   C. 3 only   E. 1 and 3 only
B. 2 only   D. 1 and 2 only

Question 31:
ATP is produced in which of the following organelles?

1. The cytoplasm
2. Plasmids
3. The mitochondria
4. The nucleus

A. 1 only   C. 3 only   E. 1 and 2
B. 2 only   D. 1 and 3

Question 32:
The cell membrane:

A. Is made up of a phospholipid bilayer which only allows active transport across it.
B. Is not found in bacteria.
C. Is a semi-permeable barrier to ions and organic molecules.
D. Consists purely of enzymes.

Question 33:
Cells of the Polyommatus atlantica butterfly of the Lycaenidae family have 446 chromosomes. Which of the following statements about a P. atlantica butterfly are correct?

1. Mitosis will produce 2 daughter cells each with 223 pairs of chromosomes
2. Meiosis will produce 4 daughter cells each with 223 chromosomes
3. Mitosis will produce 4 daughter cells each with 446 chromosomes
4. Meiosis will produce 2 daughter cells each with 223 pairs of chromosomes

A. 1 and 2 only
B. 1 and 3 only
C. 2 and 3 only
D. 3 and 4 only
E. 1, 2 and 3 only
F. 1, 2, 3 and 4

Questions 34-36 are based on the following information:
Assume that hair colour is determined by a single allele. The R allele is dominant and results in black hair. The r allele is recessive for red hair. Mary (red hair) and Bob (black hair) are having a baby girl.

Question 34:
What is the probability that the baby will have red hair?

A. 0% only
B. 25% only
C. 50% only
D. 0% or 25%
E. 0% or 50%
F. 25% or 50%

Question 35:
Mary and Bob have a second child, Tim, who is born with red hair. What does this confirm about Bob?

A. Bob is heterozygous for the red hair allele.
B. Bob is homozygous dominant for the red hair allele.
C. Bob is homozygous recessive for the red hair allele.
D. Bob does not have the red hair allele.

Question 36:
Mary and Bob go on to have a third child. What are the chances that this child will be born homozygous for black hair?

A. 0% C. 50% E. 100%
B. 25% D. 75%

Question 37:
Why does air flow into the chest on inspiration?

1. Atmospheric pressure is less than intra-thoracic pressure during inspiration.
2. Atmospheric pressure is greater than intra-thoracic pressure during inspiration.
3. Anterior and lateral chest expansion decreases absolute intra-thoracic pressure.
4. Anterior and lateral chest expansion increases absolute intra-thoracic pressure.

A. 1 only C. 2 and 3 E. 1 and 3
B. 2 only D. 1 and 4

TOUGH GCSE WORKBOOK: SCIENCE — BIOLOGY QUESTIONS

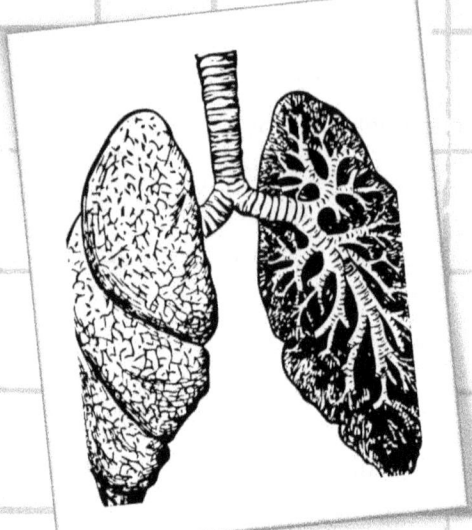

Question 38:
Which of the following components of a food chain represent the largest biomass?

A. Producers
B. Decomposers
C. Primary consumers
D. Secondary consumers
E. Tertiary consumers

Question 39:
Concerning the nitrogen cycle, which of the following are true?

1. The majority of the Earth's atmosphere is nitrogen.
2. Most of the nitrogen in the Earth's atmosphere is inert.
3. Bacteria are essential for nitrogen fixation.
4. Nitrogen fixation occurs during lightning strikes.

A. 1 and 2
B. 1 and 3
C. 2 and 3
D. 2 and 4
E. 1, 2, 3 and 4

Question 40:
Which of the following statement are correct regarding mutations?

1. Mutations always cause proteins to lose their function.
2. Mutations always change the structure of the protein encoded by the affected gene.
3. Mutations always result in cancer.

A. Only 1
B. Only 2
C. Only 3
D. 1 and 2
E. None of the above

Question 41:
Which of the following is not a function of the central nervous system?

A. Coordination of movement
B. Decision making and executive functions
C. Control of heart rate
D. Cognition
E. Memory

Question 42:
Which of the following control mechanisms is / are involved in modulating the amount of blood that is pumped per unit time?

1. Voluntary control.
2. Sympathetic control to decrease heart rate.
3. Parasympathetic control to increase heart rate.

A. Only 1
B. Only 2
C. 2 and 3
D. 1, 2 and 3
E. None of the above

Question 43:
Vijay goes to see his GP with fatty, smelly stools that float in water. Which of the following enzymes is most likely to be malfunctioning?

A. Amylase
B. Lipase
C. Protease
D. Sucrase
E. Lactase

Question 44:
Which of the following statements concerning the cardiovascular system is correct?

A. Oxygenated blood from the lungs flows to the heart via the pulmonary artery.
B. All arteries carry oxygenated blood.
C. All animals have a double circulatory system.
D. The superior vena cava contains oxygenated blood
E. None of the above.

Question 45:
In which part of the GI tract is there the least enzymatic activity for digestion?

A. Mouth
B. Stomach
C. Small intestine
D. Large intestine
E. Rectum

Question 46:
Oge touches a hot stove and immediately moves her hand away. Which of the following components are NOT involved in this reflex reaction?

1. Thermo-receptor
2. Brain
3. Spinal Cord
4. Sensory nerve
5. Motor nerve
6. Muscle

A. 1 only
B. 2 only
C. 3 only
D. 1 and 2 only
E. 1, 2 and 3 only

Question 47:
Which of the following represents a scenario with an appropriate description of the mode of transport?

1. Osmosis = water moving from a hypotonic solution outside of a potato cell, across the cell wall and cell membrane and into the hypertonic cytoplasm of the potato cell.
2. Active transport = carbon dioxide moving across a respiring cell's membrane and dissolving in blood plasma.
3. Diffusion = reabsorption of amino acids against a concentration gradient in the glomeruluar apparatus.

A. 1 only
B. 2 only
C. 3 only
D. 1 and 2 only
E. 2 and 3 only

Question 48:
Which of the following equations represents anaerobic respiration in animal cells?

1. Carbohydrate + Oxygen → Energy + Carbon dioxide + Water
2. Carbohydrate → Energy + Lactic acid + Carbon dioxide
3. Carbohydrate → Energy + Lactic acid
4. Carbohydrate → Energy + Ethanol + Carbon dioxide

A. 1 only
B. 2 and 4
C. 3 and 4 only
D. 4 only
E. 3 only

Question 49:
Which of the following statements regarding respiration in animal cells are correct?

1. Mitochondria are the centres of both aerobic and anaerobic respiration.
2. The cytoplasm is the main site of anaerobic respiration.
3. In aerobic respiration, every two moles of glucose results in the liberation of 12 moles of CO_2.
4. Anaerobic respiration is more efficient than aerobic respiration.

A. 1 and 2
B. 1 and 4
C. 2 and 3
D. 2 and 4
E. 3 and 4

Question 50:
Which of the following statements are true?

1. The nucleus contains the cell's chromosomes.
2. The cytoplasm consists purely of water.
3. The plasma membrane is a single phospholipid layer.
4. The cell wall prevents plants cells from lysis due to osmotic pressure.

A. 1 and 2
B. 1 and 4
C. 1, 3 and 4
D. 1, 2 and 3
E. 1, 2 and 4

Question 51:
Which of the following statements are true about osmosis?

1. If a medium is more concentrated than the cell cytoplasm, the cell will gain water through osmosis.
2. If a medium is less concentrated than the cell cytoplasm, the cell will gain water through osmosis.
3. If a medium is less concentrated than the cell cytoplasm, the cell will lose water through osmosis.
4. If a medium is more concentrated than the cell cytoplasm, the cell will lose water through osmosis.
5. The medium's tonicity has no impact on the movement of water.

A. 1 only
B. 2 only
C. 1 and 3
D. 2 and 4
E. 5 only

Question 52:
Which of the following statements are true about stem cells?

1. Stem cells have the ability to differentiate into other mature types of cells.
2. Stem cells are unable to maintain their undifferentiated state.
3. Stem cells can be classified as embryonic stem cells or adult stem cells.
4. Stem cells are only found in embryos.

A. 1 and 3
B. 3 and 4
C. 2 and 3
D. 1 and 2
E. 2 and 4

Question 53:
Which of the following are NOT examples of natural selection?

1. Giraffes growing longer necks to eat taller plants.
2. Antibiotic resistance developed by certain strains of bacteria.
3. Pesticide resistance among locusts in farms.
4. Breeding of horses to make them run faster.

A. 1 only
B. 4 only
C. 1 and 3
D. 1 and 4
E. 2 and 4

Question 54:
Which of the following statements are true?

1. Enzymes stabilise the transition state and therefore lower the activation energy.
2. Enzymes distort substrates in order to lower activation energy.
3. Enzymes decrease temperature to slow down reactions and lower the activation energy.
4. Enzymes provide alternative pathways for reactions to occur.

A. 1 only
B. 1 and 3
C. 1 and 4
D. 2 and 4
E. 1, 2 and 4

Question 55:
Which of the following are examples of negative feedback?

1. Salivating whilst waiting for a meal.
2. Throwing a dart.
3. The regulation of blood pH.
4. The regulation of blood pressure.

A. 1 only
B. 1 and 2
C. 3 and 4
D. 2, 3, and 4
E. 1, 2, 3 and 4

Question 56:
Which of the following statements about the immune system are true?

1. White blood cells defend against bacterial and fungal infections.
2. Red blood cells are involved in the process of phagocytosis.
3. White blood cells use antibodies to fight pathogens.
4. Antibodies are produced by bone marrow stem cells.

A. 1 and 3
B. 1 and 4
C. 2 and 3
D. 2 and 4
E. 1, 2, and 3

Question 57:
The cardiovascular system does NOT:

A. Deliver vital nutrients to peripheral cells.
B. Oxygenate blood and transport it to peripheral cells.
C. Act as a mode of transportation for hormones to reach their target organ.
D. Facilitate thermoregulation.
E. Respond to exercise by increasing the heart rate.

Question 58:
Which of the following statements is correct?

A. Adrenaline can sometimes decrease heart rate.
B. Adrenaline is rarely released during flight or fight responses.
C. Adrenaline causes peripheral vasoconstriction.
D. Adrenaline only affects the cardiovascular system.
E. Adrenaline travels primarily in lymphatic vessels.
F. None of the above.

Question 59:
Which of the following statements is true?

A. Protein synthesis occurs solely in the nucleus.
B. Each amino acid is coded for by three DNA bases.
C. Each protein is coded for by three amino acids.
D. Red blood cells can create new proteins to prolong their lifespan.
E. Protein synthesis isn't necessary for mitosis to take place.

Question 60:
A solution of amylase and carbohydrate is present in a beaker, where the pH of the contents is 6.3. Assuming amylase is saturated, which of the following will increase the rate of production of the product?

1. Add sodium bicarbonate
2. Add carbohydrate
3. Add amylase
4. Increase the temperature to 100o C

A. 1 only
B. 2 only
C. 1 and 3
D. 4 only
E. 1 and 2

Question 61:
Celestial necrosis is a newly discovered autosomal recessive disorder. A female carrier and a male with the disease produce two sons. What is the probability that neither son's genotype contains the celestial necrosis allele?

A. 100%
B. 75%
C. 50%
D. 25%
E. 0%

Question 62:
Which of the following organs has no endocrine function?

A. The thyroid
B. The ovary
C. The pancreas
D. The testes
E. None of the above.

Question 63:
Which of the following statements are true?

1. Increasing levels of insulin cause a decrease in blood glucose levels.
2. Increasing levels of glycogen cause an increase in blood glucose levels.
3. Increasing levels of adrenaline decrease the heart rate.

A. 1 only
B. 2 only
C. 3 only
D. 1 and 2
E. 2 and 3

Question 64:
Which of the following rows is correct?

	Oxygenated Blood		Deoxygenated Blood	
A.	Left atrium	Left ventricle	Right atrium	Right ventricle
B.	Left atrium	Right atrium	Left ventricle	Right ventricle
C.	Left atrium	Right ventricle	Right atrium	Right ventricle
D.	Right atrium	Right ventricle	Left atrium	Left ventricle
E.	Left ventricle	Right atrium	Left atrium	Right ventricle

Questions 65-67 are based on the following information:
The pedigree below shows the inheritance of a newly discovered disease that affects connective tissue called Nafram syndrome. Individual 1 is a normal homozygote (disease-free).

TOUGH GCSE WORKBOOK: SCIENCE

BIOLOGY QUESTIONS

Question 65:
Based on the pedigree, what is the pattern of inheritance for Nafram syndrome?

A. Autosomal dominant
B. Autosomal recessive
C. X-linked dominant
D. X-linked recessive
E. Cannot be determined

Question 66:
Which individuals in the pedigree must be heterozygous for Nafram syndrome?

A. 1 and 2
B. 8 and 9
C. 2 and 5
D. 5 and 6
E. 6 and 8

Question 67:
Taking N to denote a disease-conferring allele and n to denote a normal allele, which of the following are NOT possible genotypes for 6's parents?

1. NN x NN
2. NN x Nn
3. Nn x nn
4. Nn x Nn
5. nn x nn

A. 1 and 2
B. 1 and 3
C. 2 and 3
D. 2 and 5
E. 3 and 4

98

Question 68:
Which of the following correctly describes the passage of urine through the body?

	1st	2nd	3rd	4th
A	Kidney	Ureter	Bladder	Urethra
B	Kidney	Urethra	Bladder	Ureter
C	Urethra	Bladder	Ureter	Kidney
D	Ureter	Kidney	Bladder	Urethra

Question 69:
Which of the following best describes the passage of blood from the body, through the heart, and back to the body?

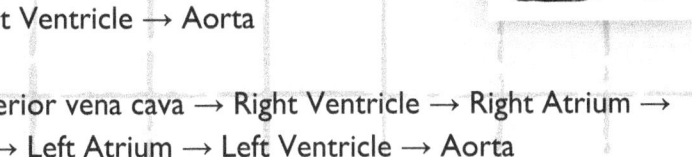

A. Aorta → Left Ventricle → Left Atrium → Inferior Vena Cava → Right Atrium → Right Ventricle → Lungs → Aorta

B. Inferior vena cava → Left Atrium → Left Ventricle → Lungs → Right Atrium → Right Ventricle → Aorta

C. Inferior vena cava → Right Ventricle → Right Atrium → Lungs → Left Atrium → Left Ventricle → Aorta

D. Aorta → Left Atrium → Left Ventricle → Lungs → Right Atrium → Right Ventricle → Inferior Vena Cava
E. None of the above.

Question 70:
Which of the following best describes the events during inspiration?

	Intrathoracic Pressure	Intercostal Muscles	Diaphragm
A	Increases	Contract	Contracts
B	Increases	Relax	Contracts
C	Increases	Contract	Relaxes
D	Increases	Relax	Relaxes
E	Decreases	Contract	Contracts

Questions 71-72 are based on the following information:
DNA is made up of four nucleotide bases: adenine, cytosine, guanine and thymine. A triplet of bases (codon) is a sequence of three nucleotides which code for an amino acid. While there are only 20 amino acids there are 64 different combinations of the four DNA nucleotide bases. This means that more than one combination of 3 DNA nucleotide sequences code for the same amino acid.

Question 71:
Which property of the genetic code is described above?

A. The code is unambiguous.
B. The code is universal.
C. The code is non-overlapping.
D. The code is degenerate.
E. The code is preserved.

Question 72:
Which type of mutation does the described property protect against the most?

A. An insertion - where a single nucleotide is inserted.
B. A point mutation - where a single nucleotide is replaced for another.
C. A deletion - where a single nucleotide is deleted.
D. A repeat expansion - where a repeated trinucleotide sequence is added.
E. A duplication - where a piece of DNA is abnormally copied.

Question 73:
Which row of the table below describes what happens when the temperature decreases in the external environment?

	Temperature Change Detected by	Sweat Gland Secretion	Cutaneous Blood Flow
A	Hypothalamus	Increases	Increases
B	Hypothalamus	Increases	Decreases
C	Hypothalamus	Decreases	Increases
D	Hypothalamus	Decreases	Decreases
E	Cerebral Cortex	Increases	Increases

Question 74:
Which of the following processes involve active transport?

1. Reabsorption of glucose in the kidney.
2. Movement of carbon dioxide into the alveoli of the lungs.
3. Movement of chemicals in a synapse.

A. 1 only
B. 2 only
C. 3 only
D. 1 and 2
E. 1 and 3

Question 75:
Which of the following statements is correct about enzymes?

A. All enzymes are made up of amino acids only.
B. Enzymes can sometimes slow the rate of reactions.
C. Enzymes are heat sensitive but resistant to changes in pH.
D. Enzymes are unspecific in their substrate use.
E. None of the above.

CHEMISTRY QUESTIONS

Question 76:
Which of the following most accurately defines an isotope?

A. An isotope is an atom of an element that has the same number of protons in the nucleus but a different number of neutrons orbiting the nucleus.
B. An isotope is an atom of an element that has the same number of neutrons in the nucleus but a different number of protons orbiting the nucleus.
C. An isotope is any atom of an element that can be split to produce nuclear energy.
D. An isotope is an atom of an element that has the same number of protons in the nucleus but a different number of neutrons in the nucleus.
E. An isotope is an atom of an element that has the same number of protons in the nucleus but a different number of electrons orbiting it.

Question 77:
Which of the following is an example of a displacement reaction?
1. $Fe + SnSO4 \rightarrow FeSO_4 + Sn$
2. $Cl_2 + 2KBr \rightarrow Br_2 + 2KCl$
3. $H_2SO_4 + Mg \rightarrow MgSO_4 + H_2$
4. $NaHCO_3 + HCl \rightarrow NaCl + CO_2 + H_2O$

A. 1 only
B. 1 and 2 only
C. 2 and 3 only
D. 3 and 4 only
E. 1, 2, 3 and 4

Question 78:
What values of **a**, **b** and **c** are needed to balance the equation below?

$$aCa(OH)_2 + bH_3PO_4 \rightarrow Ca_3(PO_4)_2 + cH_2O$$

A. a = 3, b = 2, c = 6
B. a = 2, b = 2, c = 4
C. a = 3, b = 2, c = 1
D. a = 1, b = 2, c = 3
E. a = 4, b = 2, c = 6

Question 79:
What values of **s**, **t** and **u** are needed to balance the equation below?

$$sAgNO_3 + tK_3PO_4 \rightarrow 3Ag_3PO_4 + uKNO_3$$

A. s = 9, t = 3, u = 9
B. s = 6, t = 3, u = 9
C. s = 9, t = 3, u = 6
D. s = 9, t = 6, u = 9
E. s = 3, t = 3, u = 9

Question 80:
Which of the following statements are true with regard to displacement?
1. A less reactive halogen can displace a more reactive halogen.
2. Chlorine cannot displace bromine or iodine from an aqueous solution of its salts.
3. Bromine can displace iodine according to the reactivity series.
4. Fluorine can displace chlorine as it is higher up the group.
5. Lithium can displace francium as it is higher up the group.

A. 3 only
B. 5 only
C. 1 and 2 only
D. 3 and 4 only
E. 2, 3 and 5 only

Question 81:
What mass of magnesium oxide is produced when 75g of magnesium is burned in excess oxygen?
Relative Atomic Masses: Mg = 24, O = 16

A. 80g
B. 100g
C. 125g
D. 145g
E. 175g

Question 82:
Hydrogen can combine with hydroxide ions to produce water. Which process is involved in this?

A. Hydration
B. Oxidation
C. Reduction
D. Dehydration
E. Evaporation

Question 83:
Which of the following statements about ammonia are correct?

1. It has a formula of NH_3.
2. Nitrogen contributes 82% to its mass.
3. It can be broken down again into nitrogen and hydrogen.
4. It is covalently bonded.
5. It is used to make fertilisers.

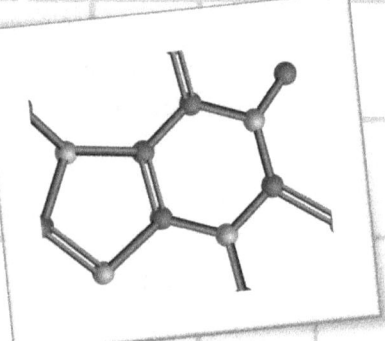

A. 1 and 2 only
B. 1 and 4 only
C. 3, 4 and 5 only
D. 1, 2 and 5 only
E. 1, 2, 3, 4 and 5

Question 84:
What colour will a universal indicator change to in a solution of whole milk (neutral pH) and lipase?

A. From green to orange.
B. From red to green.
C. From purple to green.
D. From purple to orange.
E. From yellow to purple.

Question 85:
Vitamin C [$C_6H_8O_6$] can be artificially synthesised from glucose [$C_6H_{12}O_6$]. What type of reaction is this likely to be?

A. Dehydration
B. Hydration
C. Oxidation
D. Reduction
E. Displacement

Question 86:
Which of the following statements are true?

1. Cu^{64} will undergo oxidation faster than Cu^{65}.
2. Cu^{65} will undergo reduction faster than Cu^{64}.
3. Cu^{65} and Cu^{64} have the same number of electrons.

A. 1 only
B. 2 only
C. 3 only
D. 2 and 3 only
E. 1 and 3 only
F. 1, 2 and 3

Question 87:
6g of Mg^{24} is added to a solution containing 30g of dissolved sulguric acid (H_2SO_4). Which of the following statements are true?
Relative Atomic Masses: S = 32, Mg = 24, O = 16, H = 1

1. In this reaction, the magnesium is the limiting reagent
2. In this reaction, sulfuric acid is the limiting reagent
3. The mass of salt produced equals the original mass of sulfuric acid

A. 1 only
B. 2 only
C. 3 only
D. 1 and 2 only
E. 1 and 3 only

Question 88:
In which of the following mixtures will a displacement reaction occur?

1. $Cu + 2AgNO_3$
2. $Cu + Fe(NO_3)_2$
3. $Ca + 2H_2O$
4. $Fe + Ca(OH)_2$

A. 1 only
B. 2 only
C. 3 only
D. 4 only
E. 1 and 3 only

Question 89:
Which of the following statements is true about the following chain of metals?

$Na \rightarrow Ca \rightarrow Mg \rightarrow Al \rightarrow Zn$

Moving from left to right:
1. The reactivity of the metals increases.
2. The likelihood of corrosion of the metals increases.
3. More energy is required to separate these metals from their ores.
4. The metals lose electrons more readily to form positive ions.

A. 1 and 2 only
B. 1 and 3 only
C. 2 and 3 only
D. 1 and 4 only
E. None of the above

Question 90:
In which of the following mixtures will a displacement reaction occur?

1. $I_2 + 2KBr$
2. $Cl_2 + 2NaBr$
3. $Br_2 + 2KI$

A. 1 only
B. 2 only
C. 3 only
D. 1 and 2 only
E. 2 and 3 only

Question 91:
Which of the following statements about Al and Cu are true?

1. Al is used to build aircraft because it is lightweight and resists corrosion.
2. Cu is used to build electrical wires because it is a good insulator.
3. Both Al and Cu are good conductors of heat.
4. Al is commonly alloyed with other metals to make coins.
5. Al is resistant to corrosion because of a thin layer of aluminium hydroxide on its surface.

A. 1 and 3 only
B. 1 and 4 only
C. 1, 3 and 5 only
D. 1, 3, 4, 5 only
E. 2, 4 and 5 only

Question 92:

21g of Li^7 reacts completely with excess water. Given that the molar gas volume is 24 dm^3 under the conditions, what is the volume of hydrogen produced?

A. 12 dm^3 C. 36 dm^3 E. 72 dm^3
B. 24 dm^3 D. 48 dm^3

Question 93:
Which of the following statements regarding bonding are true?

1. NaCl has stronger ionic bonds than MgCl$_2$.
2. Transition metals are able to lose varying numbers of electrons to form multiple stable positive ions.
3. All covalently bonded structures have lower melting points than ionically bonded compounds.
4. No covalently bonded structures conduct electricity.

A. 1 only   C. 3 only   E. 1 and 2 only
B. 2 only   D. 4 only

TOUGH GCSE WORKBOOK: SCIENCE — CHEMISTRY QUESTIONS

Question 94:
Consider the following two equations:

A. $C + O_2 \rightarrow CO_2$ $\Delta H = -394$ kJ per mole
B. $CaCO_3 \rightarrow CaO + CO_2$ $\Delta H = +178$ kJ per mole

Which of the following statements are true?

1. Reaction **A** is exothermic and Reaction **B** is endothermic.
2. CO_2 has less energy than C and O_2.
3. CaO is more stable than $CaCO_3$.

A. 1 only   C. 3 only   E. 1 and 3
B. 2 only   D. 1 and 2

Question 95:
Which of the following are true of regarding the oxides formed by Na, Mg and Al?

1. All of the metals and their solid oxides conduct electricity.
2. MgO has stronger bonds than Na_2O.
3. Metals are extracted from their molten ores by fractional distillation.

A. 1 only
B. 2 only
C. 3 only
D. 1 and 2 only
E. 2 and 3 only

Question 96:
Which of the following pairs have the same electronic configuration?

1. Li^+ and Na^+
2. Mg^{2+} and Ne
3. Na^{2+} and Ne
4. O^{2+} and a Carbon atom

A. 1 only
B. 1 and 2 only
C. 1 and 3 only
D. 2 and 3 only
E. 2 and 4 only

Question 97:
In relation to the reactivity of elements in Groups 1 and 2, which of the following statements is correct?

1. Reactivity decreases as you go down Group 1.
2. Reactivity increases as you go down Group 2.
3. Group 1 metals are generally less reactive than Group 2 metals.

A. Only 1
B. Only 2
C. Only 3
D. 1 and 2
E. 2 and 3

Question 98:
What role do catalysts fulfil in an endothermic reaction?

A. They increase the temperature, causing the reaction to occur at a faster rate.
B. They decrease the temperature, causing the reaction to occur at a faster rate.
C. They reduce the energy of the reactants in order to trigger the reaction.
D. They reduce the activation energy of the reaction.
E. They increase the activation energy of the reaction.

Question 99:
Tritium H^3 is an isotope of hydrogen. Why is tritium commonly referred to as 'heavy hydrogen'?

A. Because H^3 contains 3 protons making it heavier than H^1 that contains 1 proton.
B. Because H^3 contains 3 neutrons making it heavier than H^1 that contains 1 neutron.
C. Because H^3 contains 1 neutron and 2 protons making it heavier than H^1 that contains 1 neutron and 1 proton.
D. Because H^3 contains 1 proton and 2 neutrons making it heavier than H^1 that contains 1 proton.
E. Because H^3 contains 3 electrons making it heavier than H^1 that contains 1 electron.

Question 100:
In relation to redox reactions, which of the following statements are correct?

1. Oxidation describes the loss of electrons.
2. Reduction increases the electron density of an ion, atom or molecule.
3. Halogens are powerful reducing agents.

A. Only 1
B. Only 2
C. Only 3
D. 1 and 2
E. 2 and 3

Question 101:
Which one of the following statements is correct?

A. At higher temperatures, gas molecules move at angles that cause them to collide with each other more frequently.
B. Gas molecules have lower energy after colliding with each other.
C. At higher temperatures, gas molecules attract each other resulting in more collisions.
D. The average kinetic energy of gas molecules is the same for all gases at the same temperature.
E. The momentum of gas molecules decreases as pressure increases.

Question 102:
Which of the following are exothermic reactions?

1. Burning magnesium in pure oxygen
2. The combustion of hydrogen
3. Aerobic respiration
4. Evaporation of water in the oceans
5. The reaction between a strong acid and a strong base

A. 1, 2 and 4
B. 1, 2 and 5
C. 1, 3 and 5
D. 2, 3 and 4
E. 1, 2, 3 and 5

Question 103:
Ethene reacts with oxygen to produce water and carbon dioxide. Which elements are oxidised/reduced?

A. Carbon is reduced and oxygen is oxidised.
B. Hydrogen is reduced and oxygen is oxidised.
C. Carbon is oxidised and hydrogen is reduced.
D. Hydrogen is oxidised and carbon is reduced.
E. Carbon is oxidised and oxygen is reduced.

Question 104:
In the reaction between zinc and copper (II) sulphate which elements act as oxidising + reducing agents?

A. Zinc is the reducing agent while sulphur is the oxidizing agent.
B. Zinc is the reducing agent while copper in $CuSO_4$ is the oxidizing agent.
C. Copper is the reducing agent while zinc is the oxidizing agent.
D. Oxygen is the reducing agent while copper in $CuSO_4$ is the oxidizing agent.
E. Sulphur is the reducing agent while oxygen is the oxidizing agent.

Question 105:
Which of the following statements is true?

A. Acids are compounds that act as proton acceptors in an aqueous solution.
B. Acids only exist in a liquid state.
C. Strong acids are partially ionized in a solution.
D. Weak acids generally have a pH of 6 to 7.
E. The reaction between a weak and strong acid produces water and salt.

Question 106:
An unknown element, Z, has 3 isotopes: Z^5, Z^6 and Z^8. Given that the atomic mass of Z is 7, and the relative abundance of Z^5 is 20%, which of the following statements are correct?

1. Z^5 and Z^6 are present in the same abundance.
2. Z^8 is the most abundant of the isotopes.
3. Z^8 is more abundant than Z^5 and Z^6 combined.

A. 1 only
B. 2 only
C. 3 only
D. 1, 2 and 3
E. 2 and 3 only

Question 107:
Which of following best describes the products when an acid reacts with a metal that is more reactive than hydrogen?

A. Salt and hydrogen
B. Salt and ammonia
C. Salt and water
D. A weak acid and a weak base
E. A strong acid and a strong base

Question 108:

Choose an option from the table below to balance the following equation:

a $FeSO_4$ + b $K_2Cr_2O_7$ + c H_2SO_4 → d $(Fe)_2(SO_4)_3$ + e $Cr_2(SO_4)_3$ + f K_2SO_4 + g H_2O

	a	b	c	d	e	f	g
A	6	1	8	3	1	1	7
B	6	1	7	3	1	1	7
C	2	1	6	2	1	1	6
D	12	1	14	4	1	1	14
E	4	1	12	4	1	1	12

Question 109:

Which of the following statements is correct?

A. Matter consists of atoms that have a net electrical charge.
B. Atoms and ions of the same element have different numbers of protons and electrons but the same number of neutrons.
C. Over 80% of an atom's mass comes from its protons.
D. Atoms of the same element that have different numbers of neutrons react at significantly different rates.
E. Protons in the nucleus of atoms repel each other as they are positively charged.

Question 110:
Which of the following statements is correct?

A. The noble gases are chemically inert and therefore useless to man.
B. All of the noble gases have a full outer electron shell.
C. The majority of noble gases are brightly coloured.
D. The boiling point of the noble gases decreases as you progress down the Group.
E. Neon is the most abundant noble gas.

Question 111:
In relation to alkenes, which of the following statements is correct?
1. They all contain double bonds.
2. They can all be reduced to alkanes.
3. The equation 'alkene + hydrogen → alkane' is an example of a hydration reaction.

A. Only 1
B. Only 2
C. Only 3
D. 1 and 2
E. 2 and 3

Question 112:
Chlorine is made up of two isotopes, Cl^{35} (atomic mass 34.969) and Cl^{37} (atomic mass 36.966). Given that the atomic mass of chlorine is 35.453, which of the following statements is correct?

A. Cl^{35} is about 3 times more abundant than Cl^{37}.
B. Cl^{35} is about 10 times more abundant than Cl^{37}.
C. Cl^{37} is about 3 times more abundant than Cl^{35}.
D. Cl^{37} is about 10 times more abundant than Cl^{35}.
E. Both isotopes are equally abundant.

Question 113:
Which of the following statements regarding transition metals is correct?

A. Transition metals form ions that have multiple colours.
B. Transition metals usually form covalent bonds.
C. Transition metals cannot be used as catalysts as they are too reactive.
D. Transition metals are poor conductors of electricity.
E. Transition metals are found in group 2 of the periodic table.

Question 114:
20 g of impure Na^{23} reacts completely with excess water to produce 8,000 cm³ of hydrogen gas under standard conditions. What is the percentage purity of sodium?
[Under standard conditions 1 mole of gas occupies 24 dm³]

A. 88.0%
B. 76.5%
C. 66.0%
D. 38.0%
E. 15.3%

Question 115:
An organic molecule contains 70.6% Carbon, 5.9% Hydrogen and 23.5% Oxygen. It has a molecular mass of 136. What is its chemical formula?

A. C_4H_4O
B. C_5H_4O
C. $C_8H_8O_2$
D. $C_{10}H_8O_2$
E. $C2H2O$

Question 116:
Choose an option from the table below to balance the following equation:

$aS + bHNO_3 \rightarrow cH_2SO_4 + dNO_2 + eH_2O$

	a	b	c	d	e
A	3	5	3	5	1
B	1	6	1	6	2
C	6	14	6	14	2
D	2	4	2	4	4
E	2	3	2	3	2

Question 117:
Which of the following statements is true?
1. Ethane and ethene can both dissolve in organic solvents.
2. Ethane and ethene can both be hydrogenated in the presence of nickel.
3. Breaking C=C requires double the energy needed to break C-C.

A. 1 only
B. 2 only
C. 3 only
D. 1 and 2 only
E. 2 and 3 only

Question 118:

Diamond, graphite, methane and ammonia all contain covalent bonds. Which row in the table adequately describes the properties associated with each compound?

Compound	Melting Point	Able to conduct electricity	Soluble in water
1. Diamond	High	Yes	No
2. Graphite	High	Yes	No
3. $CH_{4\,(g)}$	Low	No	No
4. $NH_{3\,(g)}$	Low	No	Yes

A. 1 and 2 only
B. 2 and 3 only
C. 1 and 3 only
D. 1 and 4 only
E. 2, 3 and 4

Question 119:

Which of the following statements about catalysts are true?
1. Catalysts reduce the energy required for a reaction to take place.
2. Catalysts are used up in reactions.
3. Catalysed reactions are almost always exothermic.

A. 1 only
B. 2 only
C. 1 and 2
D. 2 and 3
E. 1, 2 and 3

Question 120:
What is the name of the molecule below?

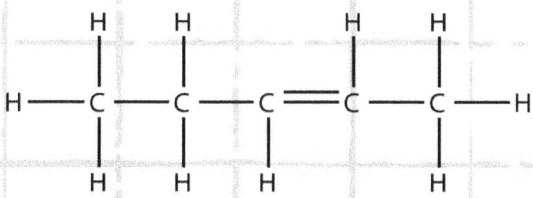

A. But-1-ene
B. But-2-ene
C. Pent-3-ene
D. Pent-1-ene
E. Pent-2-ene
F. Pentane
G. Pentanoic acid

Question 121:
Which of the following statements is correct regarding Group 1 elements? [Excluding hydrogen]

A. The oxidation number of Group 1 elements usually decreases in most reactions.
B. Reactivity decreases as you progress down Group 1.
C. Group 1 elements do not react with water.
D. All Group 1 elements react spontaneously with oxygen.
E. All of the above.
F. None of the above.

Question 122:
Which of the following statements about electrolysis are correct?

1. The cathode attracts negatively charged ions.
2. Atoms are reduced at the anode.
3. Electrolysis can be used to separate mixtures.

A. Only 1
B. Only 2
C. 2 and 3
D. Only 3
E. None of the above

Question 123:
Which of the following is **NOT** an isomer of pentane?

A. $CH_3CH_2CH_2CH_2CH_3$
B. $CH_3C(CH_3)CH_3CH_3$
C. $CH_3(CH_2)_3CH_3$
D. $CH_3C(CH_3)_2CH_3$

Question 124:
Choose an option to balance the following equation:
$Cu + HNO_3 \rightarrow Cu(NO_3)_2 + NO + H_2O$

A. $8\ Cu + 3\ HNO_3 \rightarrow 8\ Cu(NO_3)_2 + 4\ NO + 2\ H_2O$
B. $3\ Cu + 8\ HNO_3 \rightarrow 2\ Cu(NO_3)_2 + 3\ NO + 4\ H_2O$
C. $5Cu + 7HNO_3 \rightarrow 5\ Cu(NO_3)_2 + 4\ NO + 8\ H_2O$
D. $6\ Cu + 10\ HNO_3 \rightarrow 6\ Cu(NO_3)_2 + 3\ NO + 7\ H_2O$
E. $3\ Cu + 8\ HNO_3 \rightarrow 3\ Cu(NO_3)_2 + 2\ NO + 4\ H_2O$

Question 125:
Which of the following statements regarding alkenes is correct?

A. Alkenes are an inorganic homologous series.
B. Alkenes always have three times as many hydrogen atoms as they do carbon atoms.
C. Bromine water changes from clear to brown in the presence of an alkene.
D. Alkenes are more reactive than alkanes because they are unsaturated.
E. Alkenes frequently take part in subtraction reactions.

Question 126:
Which one of the following statements is correct regarding Group 17?

A. All Group 17 elements are electrophilic and therefore form negatively charged ions.
B. The reaction between sodium and fluorine is less vigorous than sodium and iodine.
C. Some Group 17 elements are found naturally as unbonded atoms.
D. All of the above.
E. None of the above.

Question 127:
Why does the electrolysis of NaCl solution (brine) require the strict separation of the products of anode and cathode?

A. To prevent the preferential discharge of ions.
B. In order to prevent spontaneous combustion.
C. In order to prevent production of H_2.
D. In order to prevent the formation of HCl.
E. In order to avoid CO poisoning.

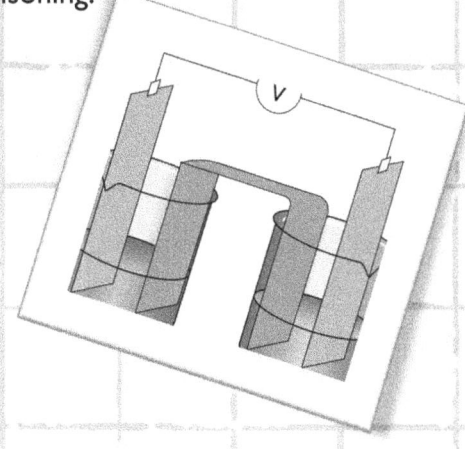

Question 128:
In relation to the electrolysis of brine (NaCl), which of the following statements are correct?

1. Electrolysis results in the production of hydrogen and chlorine gas.
2. Electrolysis results in the production of sodium hydroxide.
3. Hydrogen gas is released at the anode and chlorine gas is released at the cathode.

A. Only 1
B. Only 2
C. Only 3
D. 1 and 2
E. 1 and 3

Question 129:
Which of the following statements is correct?

A. Alkanes consist of multiple C-H bonds that are very weak.
B. An alkane with 14 hydrogen atoms is called heptane.
C. All alkanes consist purely of hydrogen and carbon atoms.
D. Alkanes burn in excess oxygen to produce carbon monoxide and water.
E. Bromine water is decolourised in the presence of an alkane.

Question 130:
Which of the following statements are correct?

1. All alcohols contain a hydroxyl functional group.
2. Alcohols are highly soluble in water.
3. Alcohols are sometimes used as biofuels.

A. Only 1
B. Only 2
C. Only 3
D. 1 and 2
E. 1, 2 and 3

Question 131:
Which row of the table below is correct?

	Non-Reducible Hydrocarbon			Reducible Hydrocarbon		
A	C_nH_{2n}	$Br_{2(aq)}$ remains brown	Saturated	C_nH_{2n+2}	Turns $Br_{2(aq)}$ colourless	Unsaturated
B	C_nH_{2n+2}	Turns $Br_{2(aq)}$ colourless	Unsaturated	C_nH_{2n}	$Br_{2(aq)}$ remains brown	Saturated
C	C_nH_{2n}	$Br_{2(aq)}$ remains brown	Unsaturated	C_nH_{2n+2}	Turns $Br_{2(aq)}$ colourless	Saturated
D	C_nH_{2n+2}	Turns $Br_{2(aq)}$ colourless	Saturated	C_nH_{2n}	$Br_{2(aq)}$ remains brown	Unsaturated
E	C_nH_{2n+2}	$Br_{2(aq)}$ remains brown	Saturated	C_nH_{2n}	Turns $Br_{2(aq)}$ colourless	Unsaturated

Question 132:
How many grams of magnesium chloride are formed when 10 grams of magnesium oxide are dissolved in excess hydrochloric acid? Relative atomic masses: Mg = 24, O = 16, H = 1, Cl = 35.5

A. 10.00
B. 14.95
C. 20.00
D. 23.75
E. 47.55

Question 133:
Pentadecane has the molecular formula $C_{15}H_{32}$. Which one of the following statements is true?

A. Pentadecane has a lower boiling point than pentane.
B. Pentadecane is more flammable than pentane.
C. Pentadecane is more volatile than pentane.
D. Pentadecane is more viscous than pentane.
E. All of the above.

Question 134:
The rate of reaction is normally dependent upon:

1. The temperature.
2. The concentration of reactants.
3. The concentration of the catalyst.
4. The surface area of the catalyst.

A. 1 and 2
B. 2 and 3
C. 2, 3 and 4
D. 1, 3 and 4
E. 1, 2, 3 and 4

Question 135:
The equation below shows the complete combustion of a sample of unknown hydrocarbon in excess oxygen.

$C_aH_b + O_2 \rightarrow cCO_2 + dH_2O$

The reaction yielded 176 grams of CO_2 and 108 grams of H_2O. What is the most likely formula of the unknown hydrocarbon? Relative atomic masses:

H = 1, C = 12, O = 16.

A. CH_4
B. CH_3
C. C_2H_6
D. C_3H_9
E. C_2H_4

Question 136:
What type of reaction must ethanol undergo in order to be converted to ethylene oxide (C_2H_4O)?

A. Oxidation
B. Reduction
C. Dehydration
D. Hydration
E. Redox

Question 137:
What values of a, b and c balance the equation below?

$a\ Ba_3N_2 + 6H_2O \rightarrow b\ Ba(OH)_2 + c\ NH_3$

	a	b	c
A	1	2	3
B	1	3	2
C	2	1	3
D	2	3	1
E	3	1	2

Question 138:
What values of a, b and c balance the equation below?

$$a\, FeS + 7O_2 \rightarrow b\, Fe_2O_3 + c\, SO_2$$

	a	b	c
A	3	2	2
B	2	4	1
C	3	1	5
D	4	1	3
E	4	2	4

Question 139:
Magnesium consists of 3 isotopes: Mg^{23}, Mg^{25}, and Mg^{26} which are found naturally in a ratio of 80:10:10.
Calculate the relative atomic mass of magnesium.

A. 23.3
B. 23.4
C. 23.5
D. 23.6
E. 24.6

Question 140:
Consider the three reactions:
1. $Cl_2 + 2Br^- \rightarrow 2Cl^- + Br_2$
2. $Cu^{2+} + Mg \rightarrow Cu + Mg^{2+}$
3. $Fe_2O_3 + 3CO \rightarrow 2Fe + 3CO_2$

Which of the following statements are correct?

A. Cl_2 and Fe_2O_3 are reducing agents.
B. CO and Cu^{2+} are oxidising agents.
C. Br_2 is a stronger oxidising agent than Cl_2.
D. Mg is a stronger reducing agent than Cu.

Question 141:
Which row of the table below best describes the properties of NaCl?

	Melting Point	Solubility in Water	Conducts electricity?	
			As a solid	In solution
A	High	Yes	Yes	Yes
B	High	No	Yes	No
C	High	Yes	No	Yes
D	High	No	No	No
E	Low	Yes	Yes	Yes

Question 142:
80g of sodium hydroxide reacts with excess zinc nitrate to produce zinc hydroxide. Calculate the mass of zinc hydroxide produced. Relative atomic mass: N = 14, Zn = 65, O = 16, Na = 23.

A. 49g
B. 95g
C. 99g
D. 100g
E. 198g

Question 143:
Which of the following statements is correct?

A. The reaction between all Group 1 metals and water is exothermic.
B. Sodium reacts less vigorously with water than potassium does.
C. All Group 1 metals react with water to produce elemental hydrogen.
D. All Group 1 metals react with water to produce a metal hydroxide.
E. All of the above.

Question 144:
Which one of the following statements is correct?

A. NaCl can be separated using sieves.
B. CO_2 can be separated using electrolysis.
C. Dyes in a sample of ink can be separated using chromatography.
D. Oil and water can be separated using fractional distillation.
E. Methane and diesel can be separated using a separating funnel.

Question 145:
Which of the following statements about the reaction between caesium and fluoride are correct?

1. It is an exothermic reaction and therefore requires catalysts.
2. It results in the formation of a salt.
3. The addition of water will make the reaction safer.

A. Only 1
B. Only 2
C. Only 3
D. 1 and 2
E. 2 and 3

Question 146:
Which of the following statements is generally true about stable isotopes?

1. The nucleus contains an equal number of neutrons and protons.
2. The nuclear charge is equal and opposite to the peripheral charge due to the orbiting electrons.
3. They can all undergo radioactive decay into more stable isotopes.

A. Only 1
B. Only 2
C. Only 3
D. 1 and 2
E. 2 and 3

Question 147:
Why do most salts have very high melting points?

A. Their surface is able to radiate away a significant portion of the heat to their environment.
B. The ionic bonds holding them together are very strong.
C. The covalent bonds holding them together are very strong.
D. They tend to form large macromolecules as each salt molecule bonds with multiple other molecules.
E. All of the above.

Question 148:
A bottle of water contains 306ml of pure deionised water. How many protons are in the bottle from the water?
[Avogadro Constant = 6×10^{23} mol^{-1}]

A. 1×10^{22}
B. 1×10^{23}
C. 1×10^{24}
D. 1×10^{25}
E. 1×10^{26}

Question 149:

On analysis, an organic substance is found to contain 41.4% carbon, 55.2% oxygen and 3.45% hydrogen by mass. Which of the following could be the empirical formula of this substance?

A. $C_3O_3H_6$

B. $C_3O_3H_{12}$

C. $C_4O_2H_4$

D. $C_4O_4H_4$

E. More information needed

Question 150:

A is a Group 2 element and B is a Group 17 element. Which row best describes what happens when A reacts with B?

	B is	Formula
A	Reduced	AB
B	Reduced	A_2B
C	Reduced	AB_2
D	Oxidised	AB
E	Oxidised	A_2B

Physics Questions

Question 151:
Which one of the following statements is **FALSE**?

A. Electromagnetic waves cause things to heat up.
B. X-rays and gamma rays can knock electrons out of their orbits.
C. Loud sounds can make objects vibrate.
D. Wave power can be used to generate electricity.
E. The amplitude of a wave determines its mass.

Question 152:
A spacecraft is analysing a newly discovered exoplanet. A rock of unknown mass falls on the planet from a height of 30 m. Given that $g = 5.4$ ms^{-2} on the planet, calculate the speed of the rock when it hits the ground and the time it took to fall.

	Speed (ms^{-1})	Time (s)
A	18	3.3
B	18	3.1
C	12	3.3
D	10	3.7
E	9	2.3

Question 153:
A canoe floating on the sea rises and falls 7 times in 49 seconds. The waves pass it at a speed of 5 ms^{-1}. How long are the waves?

A. 12 m
B. 22 m
C. 25 m
D. 35 m
E. 57 m

Question 154:
Miss Orrell lifts her 37.5 kg bike for a distance of 1.3 m in 5 s. The acceleration of free fall is 10 ms^{-2}. What is the average power that she generates?

A. 9.8 W
B. 12.9 W
C. 57.9 W
D. 79.5 W
E. 97.5 W

Question 155:
A truck accelerates at 5.6 ms^{-2} from rest for 8 seconds. Calculate the final speed and the distance travelled in 8 seconds.

	Final Speed (ms^{-1})	Distance (m)
A	40.8	119.2
B	40.8	129.6
C	42.8	179.2
D	44.1	139.2
E	44.8	179.2

Question 156:
Which of the following statements is true when a skydiver jumps out of a plane?

A. The skydiver leaves the plane and will accelerate until the air resistance is greater than their weight.
B. The skydiver leaves the plane and will accelerate until the air resistance is less than their weight.
C. The skydiver leaves the plane and will accelerate until the air resistance equals their weight.
D. The skydiver leaves the plane and will accelerate until the air resistance equals their weight squared.
E. The skydiver will travel at a constant velocity after leaving the plane.

Question 157:
A 100 g apple falls on Isaac's head from a height of 20 m. Calculate the apple's momentum before the point of impact.
Take $g = 10$ ms^{-2}

A. 0.1 kgms^{-1}
B. 0.2 kgms^{-1}
C. 1 kgms^{-1}
D. 2 kgms^{-1}
E. 10 kgms^{-1}

Question 158:
Which of the following characteristics do all electromagnetic waves all have in common?

1. They can travel through a vacuum.
2. They can be reflected.
3. They are the same length.
4. They have the same amount of energy.

A. 1, 2 and 3 only
B. 1, 2, 3 and 4 only
C. 4 and 5 only
D. 3 and 4 only
E. 1 and 2 only

Question 159:
A battery with an internal resistance of 0.8 Ω and e.m.f of 36 V is used to power a drill with resistance 1 Ω. What is the current in the circuit when the drill is connected to the power supply?

A. 5 A
B. 10 A
C. 15 A
D. 20 A
E. 25 A
F. 30 A

Question 160:
Officer Bailey throws a 20 g dart at a speed of 100 ms^{-1}. It strikes the dartboard and is brought to rest in 10 milliseconds. Calculate the average force exerted on the dart by the dartboard.

A. 0.2 N
B. 2 N
C. 20 N
D. 200 N
E. 2,000 N
F. 20,000 N

Question 161:
Professor Huang lifts a 50 kg bag through a distance of 0.7 m in 3 s. What average power does she generate to 3 significant figures? Take $g = 10ms^{-2}$

A. 113 W
B. 114 W
C. 115 W
D. 116 W
E. 117 W

Question 162:
An electric scooter is travelling at a speed of 30 ms^{-1} and is kept going at a constant speed against a 50 N frictional force by a driving force of 300 N in the direction of motion. Given that the engine runs at 200 V, calculate the current in the scooter.

A. 4.5 A
B. 45 A
C. 450 A
D. 4,500 A
E. 45,000 A

Question 163:
Which of the following statements about the physical definition of work are correct?

1. $Work\ done = \dfrac{Force}{distance}$
2. The unit of work is equivalent to kgms^{-2}.
3. Work is defined as a force causing displacement of the body upon which it acts.

A. Only 1
B. Only 2
C. Only 3
D. 1 and 2
E. 2 and 3

Question 164:
Which of the following statements about kinetic energy are correct?

1. It is defined as $E_k = \dfrac{mv^2}{2}$
2. The unit of kinetic energy is equivalent to Pa x m³.
3. Kinetic energy is equal to the amount of energy needed to decelerate the body in question from its current speed.

A. Only 1
B. Only 2
C. 2 and 3
D. 1 and 3
E. 1, 2 and 3

Question 165:
In relation to radiation, which of the following statements is **FALSE**?

A. Radiation is the emission of energy from a substance in the form of waves or particles.
B. Radiation can be either ionizing or non-ionizing.
C. Gamma radiation has very high energy.
D. Alpha radiation is of higher energy than beta radiation.
E. X-rays are an example of wave radiation.

TOUGH GCSE WORKBOOK: SCIENCE — PHYSICS QUESTIONS

Question 166:
In relation to the physical definition of half-life, which of the following statements are correct?

1. In radioactive decay, the half-life is independent of atom type and isotope.
2. Half-life is defined as the time required for exactly half of the entities to decay.
3. Half-life applies to situations of both exponential and non-exponential decay.

A. Only 1
B. Only 2
C. Only 3
D. 1 and 2
E. 2 and 3
F. 1 and 3

Question 167:
A radioactive element has a half life of 24 days. After 192 days, it has a count rate of 56.
What was the original count rate?

A. 7,168
B. 14,280
C. 14,336
D. 28,672
E. 43,008

Question 168:
Which of the following statements concerning radioactive decay is / are true?

1. As a material decays, the rate of decay decreases.
2. All nuclei of the same element will have the same half-life, as it is an innate quality of an element.
3. Radioactive decay is a highly predictable process

A. Only 1
B. Only 2
C. Only 3
D. 1 and 2
E. 2 and 3

Question 169:
Two identical resistors (R_a and R_b) are connected in a series circuit. Which of the following statements are true?

1. The current through both resistors is the same.
2. The voltage through both resistors is the same.
3. The voltage across the two resistors is given by Ohm's Law.

A. Only 1
B. Only 2
C. Only 3
D. 1 and 2
E. 1, 2 and 3

Question 170:
The sun is 8 light-minutes away from the earth. Estimate the circumference of the earth's orbit around the sun. Assume that the earth is in a circular orbit around the sun. Speed of light = 3×10^8 ms^{-1}

A. 10^{24} m
B. 10^{21} m
C. 10^{18} m
D. 10^{15} m
E. 10^{12} m

Question 171:
Which of the following statements about calculating speed are true?

1. Speed is the same as velocity.
2. The internationally standardised unit for speed is ms^{-2}.
3. Velocity = distance/time.

A. Only 1
B. 1 and 2
C. Only 2
D. Only 3
E. None of the above

Question 172:
Which of the following statements best defines Ohm's Law?

A. The current passing through an insulator between two points is indirectly proportional to the potential difference across the two points.
B. The current passing through an insulator between two points is directly proportional to the potential difference across the two points.
C. The current passing through a conductor between two points is inversely proportional to the potential difference across the two points.
D. The current passing through a conductor between two points is proportional to the square of the potential difference across the two points.
E. The current passing through a conductor between two points is directly proportional to the potential difference across the two points.

Question 173:
Which of the following statements regarding Newton's Second Law are correct?
1. For objects at rest, the resultant force must be 0 Newtons
2. Force = Mass x Acceleration
3. Force = Rate of change of Momentum

A. Only 1
B. 2 and 3
C. 1 and 3
D. 1 and 2
E. 1, 2 and 3

Question 174:
Which of the following equations concerning electrical circuits are correct?

1. $Charge = \dfrac{Voltage \times time}{Resistance}$
2. $Charge = \dfrac{Power \times time}{Voltage}$
3. $Charge = \dfrac{Current \times time}{Resistance}$

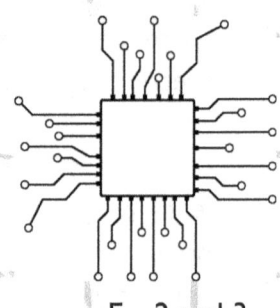

A. Only 1
B. Only 2
C. Only 3
D. 1 and 2
E. 2 and 3

Question 175:
An elevator has a mass of 1,600 kg and is carrying passengers that have a combined mass of 200 kg. A constant frictional force of 4,000 N retards its motion upward. What force must the motor provide for the elevator to move with an upward acceleration of 1 ms^{-2}? Assume: g = 10 ms^{-2}

A. 1,190 N
B. 11,900 N
C. 18,000 N
D. 22,000 N
E. 23,800 N

Question 176:
A 1,000 kg car accelerates from rest at 5 ms^{-2} for 10 s. Then, a braking force is applied to bring it to rest within 20 seconds. What is the total distance travelled by the car?

A. 125 m
B. 250 m
C. 650 m
D. 750 m
E. More information needed

Question 177:
An electric heater is connected to 120 V mains by a copper wire that has a resistance of 8 ohms. What is the power of the heater?

A. 90W
B. 180W
C. 900W
D. 1800W
E. More information needed

Question 178:
In a particle accelerator, electrons are accelerated through a potential difference of 40 MV and emerge with an energy of 40MeV (1 MeV = 1.60×10^{-13} J). Each pulse contains 5,000 electrons. The current is zero between pulses. Assuming that the electrons have zero energy prior to being accelerated what is the power delivered by the electron beam?

A. 1 kW
B. 10 kW
C. 100 kW
D. 1,000 kW
E. More information needed

Question 179:
Which **one** of the following statements is **true**?

A. When an object is in equilibrium with its surroundings, there is no energy transferred to or from the object and so its temperature remains constant.
B. When an object is in equilibrium with its surroundings, it radiates and absorbs energy at the same rate and so its temperature remains constant.
C. Radiation is faster than convection but slower than conduction.
D. Radiation is faster than conduction but slower than convection.
E. None of the above.

Question 180:
A 6kg block is pulled from rest along a horizontal frictionless surface by a constant horizontal force of 12 N. Calculate the speed of the block after it has moved 300 cm.

A. $2\sqrt{3}\ ms^{-1}$
B. $4\sqrt{3}\ ms^{-1}$
C. $4\sqrt{3}\ ms^{-1}$
D. $12\ ms^{-1}$
E. $\sqrt{\frac{3}{2}}\ ms^{-1}$

Question 181:
A 100 V heater heats 1.5 litres of pure water from 10°C to 50°C in 50 minutes. Given that 1 kg of pure water requires 4,000 J to raise its temperature by 1°C, calculate the resistance of the heater.

A. 12.5 ohms
B. 25 ohms
C. 125 ohms
D. 250 ohms
E. 500 ohms

TOUGH GCSE WORKBOOK: SCIENCE — PHYSICS QUESTIONS

Question 182:
Which of the following statements are **true**?

1. The half life of a radioactive substance is equal to half the time taken for its nuclei to decay.
2. When a nucleus emits a beta particle, it is converted to a new element.
3. When a nucleus emits an alpha particle, one of its neutrons becomes a proton and an electron.

A. Only 1
B. 2 and 3
C. 2 only
D. 1 and 2
E. None of the above

Question 183:
Which of the following statements are **true**? Assume $g = 10$ ms^{-2}.

1. Gravitational potential energy is defined as $\Delta E_p = m \times g \times \Delta h$.
2. Gravitational potential energy is a measure of the work done against gravity.
3. A reservoir situated 1 km above ground level with 10^6 litres of water has a potential energy of 1 Giga Joule.

A. Only 1
B. Only 2
C. Only 3
D. 1 and 3
E. 1, 2 and 3

Question 184:
Which of the following statements are correct in relation to Newton's 3rd law?

1. For every action there is an equal and opposite reaction.
2. According to Newton's 3rd law, there are no isolated forces.
3. When a rifle recoils as a bullet is fired from it, according to Newton's third law of motion, the acceleration of the recoiling rifle is the same size as the acceleration of the bullet.

A. Only 1
B. Only 2
C. 2 and 3
D. 1 and 2
E. 1, 2 and 3

Question 185:
Which of the following statements are correct?
1. Positively charged objects have gained electrons.
2. Electrical charge in a circuit over a period of time can be calculated if the voltage and resistance are known.
   Objects can be charged by friction.

A. Only 1
B. Only 2
C. Only 3
D. 1 and 2
E. 2 and 3
F. 1 and 3
G. 1, 2 and 3

Question 186:
Which of the following statements is true?

A. The gravitational force between two objects is independent of their mass.
B. Each planet in the solar system exerts a gravitational force on the Earth.
C. Two objects dropped from the Eiffel tower will always land on the ground at the same time if they have the same mass.
D. All of the above.
E. None of the above.

Question 187:
Which of the following best defines an electrical conductor?

A. Conductors are usually made from metals, and they conduct electrical charge in multiple directions.
B. Conductors are usually made from non-metals, and they conduct electrical charge in multiple directions.
C. Conductors are usually made from metals, and they conduct electrical charge in one fixed direction.
D. Conductors are usually made from non-metals, and they conduct electrical charge in one fixed direction.
E. Conductors allow the passage of electrical charge with zero resistance because they contain freely mobile charged particles.

Question 188:

An 800 kg compact car delivers 20% of its power output to its wheels. If the car has a mileage of 30 miles/gallon and travels at a speed of 60 miles/hour, how much power is delivered to the wheels? 1 gallon of petrol contains 9×10^8 J.

A. 10 kW
B. 20 kW
C. 40 kW
D. 50 kW
E. 100 kW

Question 189:

Which of the following statements about beta radiation are true?

1. After a beta particle is emitted, the atomic mass number is unchanged.
2. Beta radiation can penetrate paper but not aluminium foil.
3. A beta particle is emitted from the nucleus of the atom when an electron transforms to a neutron.

A. 1 only
B. 2 only
C. 1 and 3
D. 1 and 2
E. 2 and 3
F. 1, 2 and 3

Question 190:

A car with a weight of 15,000 N is travelling at a speed of 15 ms^{-1} when it crashes into a wall and is brought to rest in 10 milliseconds. Calculate the average braking force exerted on the car by the wall. Take $g = 10$ ms^{-2}

A. $1.25 \times 10^4 N$
B. $1.25 \times 10^5 N$
C. $1.25 \times 10^6 N$
D. $2.25 \times 10^4 N$
E. $2.25 \times 10^6 N$

Question 191:
Which of the following statements are correct?

1. Electrical insulators are usually metals e.g. copper.
2. The flow of charge through electrical insulators is extremely low.
3. Electrical insulators can be charged by rubbing them together.

A. Only 1
B. Only 2
C. Only 3
D. 1 and 2
E. 2 and 3

The following information is needed for Questions 192 and 193:

This graph represents a car's movement. At t=0 the car's displacement was 0 m.

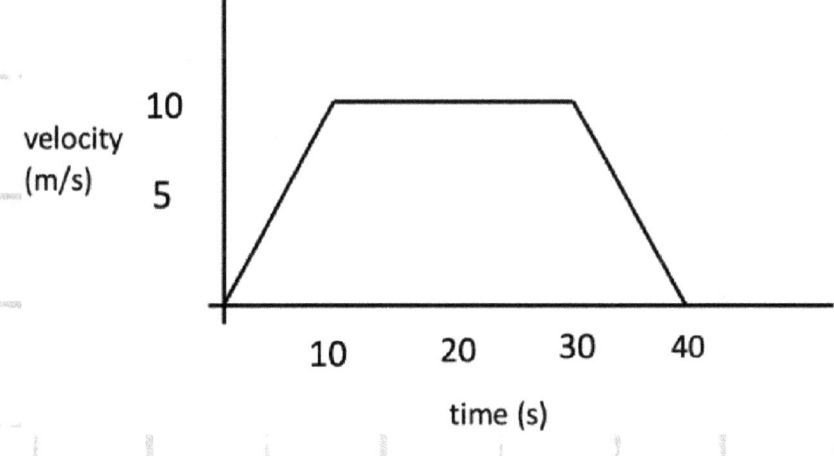

Question 192:
Which of the following statements are **NOT** true?

1. The car is reversing after t = 30.
2. The car moves with constant acceleration from t = 0 to t = 10.
3. The car moves with constant speed from t = 10 to t = 30.

A. 1 only
B. 2 only
C. 3 only
D. 1 and 3
E. 1 and 2

Question 193:
Calculate the distance travelled by the car.

A. 200 m
B. 300 m
C. 350 m
D. 400 m
E. More information needed

Question 194:
A 1,000 kg rocket is launched during a thunderstorm and reaches a constant velocity 30 seconds after launch. Suddenly, a strong gust of wind acts on the rocket for 5 seconds with a force of 10,000 N in the direction of movement.
What is the resulting change in velocity?

A. 0.5 ms^{-1}
B. 5 ms^{-1}
C. 50 ms^{-1}
D. 500 ms^{-1}
E. More information needed

Question 195:
A 0.5 tonne crane lifts a 0.01 tonne wardrobe by 100 cm in 5,000 milliseconds.
Calculate the average power generated by the crane. Take $g = 10$ ms^{-2}.

A. 0.2 W
B. 2 W
C. 5 W
D. 20 W
E. More information needed

Question 196:
A 20 V battery is connected to a circuit consisting of a 1 Ω and 2 Ω resistor in parallel. Calculate the overall current of the circuit.

A. 6.67 A
B. 8 A
C. 12 A
D. 20 A
E. 30 A

Question 197:
Which **one** of the following statements is correct?

A. The speed of light changes when it enters water.
B. The speed of light changes when it leaves water.
C. The direction of light changes when it enters water.
D. The direction of light changes when it leaves water.
E. All of the above.
F. None of the above.

Question 198:

In a parallel circuit, a 60 V battery is connected to two branches. Branch A contains 6 identical 5 Ω resistors and branch B contains 2 identical 10 Ω resistors.

Calculate the current in branches A and B.

	I_A (A)	I_B (A)
A	0	6
B	6	0
C	2	3
D	3	2
E	1	5

Question 199:

Calculate the voltage of an electrical circuit that has a power output of 50,000,000,000 nW and a current of 0.000000004 GA.

A. 0.0125 GV
B. 0.0125 MV
C. 0.0125 kV
D. 0.0125 nV
E. 0.0125 mV

Question 200:
Which of the following statements about radioactive decay is correct?

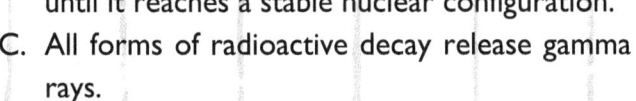

A. Radioactive decay is highly predictable.
B. An unstable element will continue to decay until it reaches a stable nuclear configuration.
C. All forms of radioactive decay release gamma rays.
D. All forms of radioactive decay release X-rays.
E. None of the above.

Question 201:
A circuit contains three identical resistors of unknown resistance connected in series with a 15 V battery. The power output of the circuit is 60 W.
Calculate the overall resistance of the circuit when two further identical resistors are added to it.

A. 0.125 Ω
B. 1.25 Ω
C. 3.75 Ω
D. 6.25 Ω
E. 18.75 Ω

Question 202:
The engine in a 5,000 kg tractor uses 1 litre of fuel to move 0.1 km. 1 ml of the fuel contains 20 kJ of energy.
Calculate the engine's efficiency. Take $g = 10$ ms^{-2}

A. 2.5 %
B. 25 %
C. 38 %
D. 50 %
E. More information needed.

Question 203:
Which of the following statements are correct?

1. Electromagnetic induction occurs when a wire moves relative to a magnet.
2. Electromagnetic induction occurs when a magnetic field changes.
3. An electrical current is generated when a coil rotates in a magnetic field.

A. Only 1
B. 1 and 3
C. 2 and 3
D. 1 and 2
E. 1, 2 and 3

Question 204:
Which of the following statements are correct regarding parallel circuits?

1. The current flowing through a branch is dependent on the resistance of that branch.
2. The total current flowing into the branches is equal to the total current flowing out of the branches.
3. An ammeter will always give the same reading regardless of its location in the circuit.

A. Only 1
B. Only 2
C. 2 and 3
D. 1 and 2
E. All of the above

Question 205:
Which of the following statements regarding series circuits are true?

1. The overall resistance of a circuit is given by the sum of all resistors in the circuit.
2. Electrical current moves from the positive terminal to the negative terminal.
3. Electrons move from the positive terminal to the negative terminal.

A. Only 1
B. Only 2
C. Only 3
D. 1 and 2
E. 1 and 3

Question 206:
The graphs below show current vs. voltage plots for 4 different electrical components.

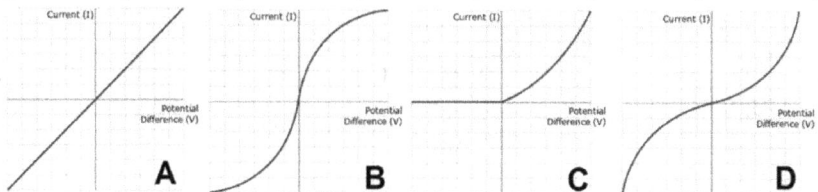

Which of the following graphs represents a resistor at constant temperature, and which represents a filament lamp?

	Fixed Resistor	Filament Lamp
A	A	B
B	A	C
C	D	D
D	C	A
E	C	C

Question 207:
Which of the following statements are true about vectors?

A. Vectors can be added or subtracted.
B. All vector quantities have a defined magnitude.
C. All vector quantities have a defined direction.
D. All of the above.
E. None of the above.

Question 208:
The acceleration due to gravity on the Earth is six times greater than that on the moon. Dr Tyson records the weight of a rock as 250 N on the moon.

Calculate the density of the rock given that it has a volume of 250 cm³. Take g_{Earth} = 10 ms^{-2}

A. 0.2 kg/cm³
B. 0.5 kg/cm³
C. 0.6 kg/cm³
D. 0.7 kg/cm³
E. More information needed.

Question 209:
A radioactive element X^{225}_{78} undergoes alpha decay. What is the atomic mass and atomic number after 5 alpha particles have been released?

	Mass Number	Atomic Number
A	200	56
B	200	58
C	215	64
D	205	68
E	215	58

Question 210:

A 20 A current passes through a circuit with resistance of 10 Ω. The circuit is connected to a transformer that contains a primary coil with 5 turns and a secondary coil with 10 turns. Calculate the potential difference exiting the transformer.

A. 100 V
B. 200 V
C. 400 V
D. 500 V
E. 2,000 V

Question 211:

A metal ball of unknown mass is dropped from an altitude of 1 km and reaches terminal velocity 300 m before it hits the ground. Given that resistive forces do a total of 10 kJ of work for the last 100 m before the ball hits the ground, calculate the mass of the ball. Take $g = 10ms^{-2}$.

A. 1 kg
B. 2 kg
C. 5 kg
D. 10 kg
E. More information needed.

Question 212:

Which of the following statements about the electromagnetic spectrum is correct?

A. The wavelength of ultraviolet waves is shorter than that of x-rays.
B. For waves in the electromagnetic spectrum, wavelength is directly proportional to frequency.
C. Waves in the electromagnetic spectrum travel at the speed of sound.
D. Humans are able to visualise the majority of the electromagnetic spectrum.
E. None of the above.

Question 213:
In relation to the Doppler effect, which of the following statements are true?
1. If an object emitting a wave moves towards the sensor, the wavelength increases and frequency decreases.
2. An object that originally emitted a wave of a wavelength of 20 mm followed by a second reading delivering a wavelength of 15 mm is moving towards the sensor.
3. The faster the object is moving away from the sensor, the greater the increase in frequency.

A. Only 1
B. Only 2
C. Only 3
D. 1 and 2
E. 2 and 3

Question 214:
A 5 g bullet travels at 1 km/s and hits a brick wall. It penetrates 50 cm before being brought to rest 100 ms after impact. Calculate the average braking force exerted by the wall on the bullet.

A. 50 N
B. 500 N
C. 5,000 N
D. 50,000 N
E. More information needed.

Question 215:
Polonium (Po) is a highly radioactive element that has no known stable isotope. Po^{210} undergoes radioactive decay to Pb^{206} and Y. Calculate the number of protons in 10 moles of Y. [Avogadro's Constant = 6×10^{23} mol^{-1}]

A. 0
B. 1.2×10^{24}
C. 1.2×10^{25}
D. 2.4×10^{24}
E. 2.4×10^{25}

Question 216:

Dr Sale measures the background radiation in a nuclear wasteland to be 1,000 Bq. He then detects a spike of 16,000 Bq from a nuclear rod made up of an unknown material. 300 days later, he visits and can no longer detect a reading higher than 1,000 Bq from the rod, even though it hasn't been disturbed.

What is the longest possible half-life of the nuclear rod?

A. 25 days
B. 50 days
C. 75 days
D. 100 days
E. More information needed

Question 217:

A radioactive element Y^{200}_{89} undergoes several stages of beta (β^-) and gamma decay. What are the numbers of protons and neutrons in the element after the emission of 5 beta particles and 2 gamma waves?

	Protons	Neutrons
A	79	101
B	84	116
C	89	111
D	94	111
E	94	106

Question 218:
Most symphony orchestras tune to 'standard pitch' (frequency = 440 Hz). When they are tuning, sound directly from the orchestra reaches audience members that are 500 m away in 1.5 seconds. **Estimate** the wavelength of 'standard pitch'.

A. 0.05 m
B. 0.5 m
C. 0.75 m
D. 1.5 m
E. More information needed

Question 219:
A 1 kg cylindrical artillery shell with a radius of 50 mm is fired at a speed of 200 ms^{-1}. It strikes an armour-plated wall and is brought to rest in 500 μs.

Calculate the average pressure exerted on the artillery shell by the wall at the time of impact.

A. 5×10^6 Pa
B. 5×10^7 Pa
C. 5×10^8 Pa
D. 5×10^9 Pa
E. More information needed

Question 220:
A 1,000 W display fountain launches 120 litres of water straight up every minute. Given that the fountain is 10% efficient, calculate the maximum possible height that the stream of water could reach.
Assume that there is negligible air resistance and $g = 10$ ms^{-2}.

A. 1 m
B. 5 m
C. 10 m
D. 20 m
E. 50m

Question 221
In relation to transformers, which of the following is true?
1. Step up transformers increase the voltage leaving the transformer.
2. In step down transformers, the number of turns in the primary coil is smaller than in the secondary coil.

For transformers that are 100% efficient:
$I_p V_p = I_s V_s$

A. Only 1
B. Only 2
C. Only 3
D. 2 and 3
E. 1 and 3

Question 222:
The half-life of Carbon-14 is 5,730 years. A bone is found that contains 6.25% of the amount of C^{14} that would be found in a modern-day bone. How old is the bone?

A. 11,460 years
B. 17,190 years
C. 22,920 years
D. 28,650 years
E. 34,380 years

Question 223:
A wave has a velocity of 2,000 mm/s and a wavelength of 250 cm. What is its frequency in MHz?

A. 8×10^{-3} MHz
B. 8×10^{-4} MHz
C. 8×10^{-5} MHz
D. 8×10^{-6} MHz
E. 8×10^{-7} MHz

Question 224:
A radioactive element has a half-life of 25 days. After 350 days it has a count rate of 50. What was its original count rate?

A. 102,400
B. 162,240
C. 204,800
D. 409,600
E. 819,200

Question 225:
Which of the following units is **NOT** equivalent to a Volt (V)?

A. $JA^{-1}s^{-1}$
B. WA^{-1}
C. $Nms^{-1}A^{-1}$
D. NmC
E. $JC-1$

ANSWERS

BIOLOGY ANSWERS

Question 01: A
DNA consists of 4 bases: adenine, guanine, thymine, and cytosine. The sugar backbone consists of deoxyribose, hence the name DNA. DNA is found in the cytoplasm of prokaryotes (bacteria are prokaryotic!).

Question 02: D
1 – **correct** – Mitochondria are responsible for energy production by ATP synthesis.
2 – **incorrect** – Animal cells do not have a cell wall, only a cell membrane.
3 – **correct** – chloroplasts are only found in animal cells, they are the site of photosynthesis

Question 03: B
If you aren't studying A-level biology, this question may stretch you. However, it is possible to reach an answer by process of elimination.
A, D, E – incorrect – Mitochondria are the 'powerhouse' of the cell in aerobic respiration, responsible for cell energy production rather than DNA replication or protein synthesis.
C – incorrect - As energy producers they are required in muscle cells in large numbers.
B – correct – Hence, we can conclude that they are enveloped by a double membrane, possibly because they started out as independent prokaryotes engulfed by eukaryotic cells.

TOUGH GCSE WORKBOOK: SCIENCE — ANSWERS

Question 04: A
The majority of bacteria are commensal, thus don't lead to disease. Each of the other statements are true.

Question 05: C
Bacteria carry genetic information on plasmids and not in nuclei like animal cells. They don't need meiosis for replication, as they do not require gametes. Bacterial genomes consist of DNA, just like animal cells.

Question 06: C
Active transport requires a transport protein and ATP, as work is being done against an electrochemical gradient. Unlike diffusion, the relative concentrations of the materials being transported aren't important.

Question 07: D
Meiosis produces haploid gametes. This allows for fusion of 2 gametes to reach a full diploid set of chromosomes again in the zygote.

Question 08: B
Mendelian inheritance separates traits into dominant or recessive. It applies to all sexually reproducing organisms. Don't get confused by statement C – the offspring of 2 heterozygotes has a 25% chance of expressing a recessive trait, but it will be homozygous recessive.

TOUGH GCSE WORKBOOK: SCIENCE   ANSWERS

Question 09: A
Hormones are released into the bloodstream and act on receptors in different organs in order to cause relatively slow changes to the body's physiology. Hormones frequently interact with the nervous system, e.g. adrenaline and insulin, however, they don't directly cause muscles to contract. Almost all hormones are synthesised.

Question 10: D
Neuronal signalling can happen via direct electrical stimulation of nerves or via chemical stimulation of synapses which produce a current that travels along the nerves. Electrical synapses are very rare in mammals; the majority of mammalian synapses are chemical.

Question 11: D
Remember that pH changes cause changes in electrical charge on proteins (= polypeptides) that could interfere with protein – protein interactions. Whilst the other statements are all correct to a certain extent, they are the downstream effects of what would happen if enzymes (which are also proteins) didn't work.

Question 12: A
The bacterial cell wall is made up of murein and protects the bacterium from the external environment, in particular from osmotic stresses, and is important in most bacteria.

Question 13: C
Sexual reproduction relies on formation of gametes during **meiosis**. Mitosis doesn't produce genetically distinct cells. Mitosis is, however, the basis for tissue growth.

Question 14: A
A mutation is a permanent change in the nucleotide sequence of DNA. Whilst mutations may lead to changes in organelles and chromosomes, or even be harmful, they are strictly defined as permanent changes to the DNA or RNA sequence.

Question 15: E
Mutations are fairly common, but in the vast majority of cases do not have any impact on phenotype due to the redundancy of the genome. Sometimes they can confer selective advantages and allow organisms to survive better (i.e. evolve by natural selection), or they can lead to cancers as cells start dividing uncontrollably.

Question 16: D
Antibodies represent a pivotal molecule of the immune system. They provide very pointed and selective targeting of pathogens and toxins without causing damage to the body's own cells.

Question 17: A
Kidneys are not involved in digestion, but do filter the blood of waste products. Glucose is found in high concentrations in the urine of diabetics. The lack of insulin production and/or tissue response to insulin means diabetics cannot absorb glucose and thus it must be excreted as a waste product.

Question 18: D
Hormones are slower acting than nervous signals and act for a longer time. Hormones also act in a more general way. Adrenaline is also a hormone released into the body causing the fight-or-flight response. Although it is quick acting, it still lasts for a longer time than a nervous response, as you can still feel its effects for a time after the response, e.g., shaking hands.

Question 19: D
Homeostasis is about minimising changes to the internal environment by modulating both input and output.

Question 20: B
There is less energy and biomass each time you move up a trophic level. Only 10% of consumed energy is transferred to the next trophic level, so only one tenth of the previous biomass can be sustained in the next trophic level up.

Question 21: A
In asexual reproduction, there is no fusion of gametes as the single parent cell divides. There is therefore no mixing of chromosomes and, as a result, no genetic variation.

Question 22: E
The image is first formed on the retina which conveys it to the brain via a sensory nerve. The brain then sends an impulse to the muscle via a motor neuron.

Question 23: D

1 – correct – the right-hand side of the heart contains deoxygenated blood, while the left-hand side contains oxygenated blood.

2 – incorrect – the aorta receives oxygenated blood from the left <u>ventricle</u>.

3 – incorrect – the heart pumps deoxygenated blood into the pulmonary <u>artery</u>.

4 – incorrect – valves prevent flow of blood backwards from ventricle to atrium, while walls are present to prevent flow from ventricle to ventricle (and atrium to atrium).

Question 24: E

Clones are genetically identical by definition, and a large number of them could conceivably reduce the gene pool of a population. In adult cell cloning, the genetic material of an egg is replaced with the genetic material of an adult cell. Cloning is possible for all DNA based life forms, including plants and other types of animals.

Question 25: E

Genetic variation gives rise to a variety of intraspecies phenotypes, e.g. different eye colours. If mutations confer a selective advantage, those individuals with the mutation will survive to reproduce and grow in numbers. Genetic variation is caused by a combination of parental genetic mixing and mutations. Species with similar characteristics often do have similar genes.

Question 26: E
Alleles are different versions of the same gene. If you are a homozygous for a trait, you have two identical alleles for that particular gene, and if you are heterozygous, you have two different alleles for that gene. Recessive traits only appear in the phenotype when there are no dominant alleles for that trait, i.e. two recessive alleles are carried.

Question 27: D
Remember that red blood cells don't have a nucleus and therefore have minimal DNA. In meiosis, a diploid cell divides in such a way so as to produce four haploid cells. Any type of cell division will require energy.

Question 28: C
The hypothalamus detects too little water in the blood, so the pituitary gland releases ADH. The kidneys maintain the blood water level and allow less water to be lost in the urine until the blood water level returns to normal.

Question 29: E
Venous blood has a higher level of carbon dioxide and lower level of oxygen. Carbon dioxide forms carbonic acid in aqueous solution, thus making the pH of venous blood slightly more acidic than arterial blood. This leaves only **D** and **E** as possibilities, but recall that under normal physiological conditions, pH is maintained under strict control, giving an answer of pH 7.4 as the most likely. Remember, the pH scale is logarithmic, so a pH of 8.0 would be a big difference in the number of H+ ions in the blood!

Question 30: E
1 – **correct** – the cytoplasm is 80% water.
2 – **incorrect** – the cytoplasm doesn't contain everything, e.g. DNA is found in the nucleus.
3 – **correct** – the cytoplasm contains, among other things, electrolytes and proteins.

Question 31: D
ATP is produced in mitochondria in aerobic respiration and in the cytoplasm during anaerobic respiration only.
1 – **correct** – ATP is produced in the cytoplasm during anaerobic respiration only.
2 – **incorrect** – plasmids are not a site of ATP production.
3 – **correct** – ATP is produced in the mitochondria during aerobic respiration only.
4 – **incorrect** – the nucleus is not a site of ATP production.

Question 32: C
The cell membrane allows both active transport (via specialised transport proteins) and passive transport (via diffusion) of certain ions and molecules and is found in eukaryotes and prokaryotes like bacteria. It is a phospholipid bilayer.

Question 33: A
1 and 2 only: 223 PAIRS = 446 chromosomes; meiosis produces 4 daughter cells with half of the original number of chromosomes each, while mitosis produces two daughter cells with the original number of chromosomes each.

Question 34: E
If Bob is homozygous dominant (RR) the probability of having a child with red hair is 0%. However, if Bob is heterozygous (Rr), there is a 50% chance of having a child with red hair, since Mary must be homozygous recessive (rr) to have red hair. As we do not know Bob's genotype, both possibilities must be considered.

Question 35: A
If an offspring is born with red hair, it confirms Bob is heterozygous (Rr). He cannot have a red-haired child if he is homozygous dominant (RR), and would himself have red hair were he homozygous recessive (rr).

Question 36: A
Monohybrid cross rr and Rr results in 50% Rr and 50% rr offspring. 50% of offspring will have black hair, but they will be heterozygous for the hair allele (Rr).

Question 37: C
When the chest walls expand, the intra-thoracic pressure decreases. This causes the atmospheric pressure outside the chest to be greater than pressure inside the chest, resulting in a flow of air into the chest.

Question 38: A
Producers are found at the bottom of food chains and always have the largest biomass of all the trophic levels.

Question 39: E

All the statements are true; the carbon and nitrogen cycles are examinable in Section 2, so make sure you understand them! The atmosphere is 79% inert N_2 gas, which must be 'fixed' to useable forms by high-energy lightning strikes or by bacterial mediation. Humans also manually fix nitrogen for fertilisers with the Haber process.

Question 40: E

None of the above statements are correct.

1 – incorrect – mutations can be silent, for example if the new triplet codes for the same amino acid as the original. Or, a mutation may cause a change in the amino acid, but if the amino acid is not in the active site or has similar properties to the original amino acid, this may not affect the function of the protein. Mutations can either be silent, cause loss of function, or even gain of function!

2 – incorrect – as outlined above, mutations can be silent – i.e. a substitution of one triplet codon for another that codes for the same amino acid. Or, if the mutation is in an exon (part of the protein that is cut out to make the protein functional), the structure of the end product protein won't be affected.

3 – incorrect – whilst cancer arises as a result of a series of mutations (the two-hit hypothesis), only a small percentage of mutations actually lead to cancer.

Question 41: C

Remember that heart rate is controlled via the autonomic nervous system, which isn't a part of the central nervous system.

Question 42: E
None of the above are correct. There is no voluntary input to the heart in the form of a neuronal connection. Parasympathetic neurones slow the heart and sympathetic nervous input accelerates heart rate.

Question 43: B
If lipase is not working, fat from the diet will not be broken down, and will be instead excreted in the stool. Lactase, for instance, is responsible for breaking down lactose, and its malfunctioning is the reason for lactose intolerance.

Question 44: E
None of the statements A-D are correct.
A – incorrect – oxygenated blood from the lungs flows to the heart via the pulmonary <u>vein</u>.
B – incorrect – the pulmonary artery is the exception to this rule! It carries deoxygenated blood from the heart to the lungs.
C – incorrect – some animals, such as fish, have single circulatory systems.
D – incorrect – the SVC contains deoxygenated blood, returning to the heart from the body.

Question 45: E
Enzymatic digestion takes place throughout the GI tract, including in the mouth (e.g. amylase), stomach (e.g. pepsin), and small intestine (e.g. trypsin). The large intestine is primarily responsible for water absorption, whilst the rectum acts as a temporary store for faecal matter (i.e. digestion has finished prior to the rectum).

Question 46: B

This is an example of the monosynaptic stretch reflex; these reflexes occur at the level of the spinal cord and therefore don't involve the brain. These reflexes are truly involuntary as they involve no higher processing.

Thermo-receptors are involved in the reaction – they detect the heat and send the information to a **sensory nerve**. The sensory nerve takes the information to the **spinal cord**, where the information is relayed to a **motor nerve**. The motor nerve then relays the information to a **muscle** and causes muscular contraction to remove the hand from the hot stimulus.

Question 47: A

Statement 2 describes diffusion as CO_2 is moving along the concentration gradient. Statement 3 describes active transport, as amino acids are moving against the concentration gradient.

Question 48: C

3 is the correct equation for animals, and 4 is correct for plants.

Question 49: C

The mitochondria are only the site for aerobic respiration, as anaerobic respiration occurs in the cytoplasm. Aerobic respiration produces more ATP per substrate than anaerobic respiration, and therefore is also more efficient. The chemical equation for glucose being respired aerobically is: $C_6H_{12}O_6 + 6O_2 \rightarrow 6CO_2 + 6H_2O$. Thus, the molar ratio is 1:6 (i.e. 1 mole glucose produces 6 moles of CO_2).

Question 50: B
The nucleus contains the DNA and chromosomes of the cell. The cytoplasm contains enzymes, salts, and amino acids in addition to water. The plasma membrane is a bilayer. Lastly, the cell wall is indeed responsible for protecting the cell against increased osmotic pressures.

Question 51: D
When a solution is hypotonic/less concentrated relative to the cell cytoplasm, the cell will gain water through osmosis. When the solution is isotonic, there will be no net movement of water across the cell membrane. Lastly, when the solution is hypertonic/more concentrated relative to the cell cytoplasm, the cell will lose water by osmosis.

Question 52: A
Stem cells have the ability to differentiate and so produce other kinds of cells. However, they also have the ability to generate cells of their own kind and stem cells are able to maintain their undifferentiated state. This is totipotency. The two types of stem cells are embryonic stem cells and adult stem cells. The adult stem cells are present in both children and adults.

Question 53: B
All of the following statements are examples of natural selection, except for the breeding of horses. Breeding and animal husbandry are notable methods of artificial selection, which are brought about by humans.

Question 54: C
Enzymes create a stable environment to stabilise the transition state. Enzymes do not distort substrates. Enzymes generally have little effect on temperature directly. Lastly, they are able to provide alternative pathways for reactions to occur.

Question 55: C
A negative feedback system seeks to minimise changes in a system by modulating the response in accordance with the error that's generated. Salivating before a meal is an example of a feed-forward system (i.e. salivating is an anticipatory response). Throwing a dart does not involve any feedback (during the action). pH and blood pressure are both important homeostatic variables that are controlled via powerful negative feedback mechanisms, e.g. massive haemorrhage leads to compensatory tachycardia.

Question 56: A
1 – **correct** – one of the major functions of white blood cells is to defend the body against infectious agents, including bacterial and fungal infections (viral infections too!).
2 – **incorrect** – WBCs, not RBCs, are involved in phagocytosis.
3 – **correct** – WBCs, specifically plasma cells, produce antibodies. These stick to recognition sites on pathogens and help the immune system to target these pathogens.
4 – **incorrect** – antibodies are produced by white blood cells (specifically, plasma cells, a type of B cell).

Question 57: B
A – correct – the CVS does transport nutrients, such as glucose and oxygen, to all cells in the body.
B – incorrect – the <u>respiratory</u> system is responsible for oxygenating blood.
C – correct – the CVS transports hormones to target organs.
D – correct – via vasoconstriction in response to cold, and vasodilation in response to heat, the cardiovascular system contributes to thermoregulation.
E – correct – heart rate increases in response to exercise.

Question 58: C
Adrenaline always increases heart rate and is almost always released during sympathetic responses. It travels primarily in the blood and affects multiple organ systems. It is also a potent vasoconstrictor.

Question 59: B
Protein synthesis occurs in the cytoplasm. Proteins are usually coded for by several amino acids. Red blood cells lack a nucleus and, therefore, do not contain sufficient DNA to create new proteins. Protein synthesis is a key part of mitosis, as it allows the parent cell to grow prior to division.

TOUGH GCSE WORKBOOK: SCIENCE — ANSWERS

Question 60: C
Remember that most enzymes work better in neutral environments (amylase works even better at slightly alkaline pH). Thus, adding sodium bicarbonate will increase the pH and hence increase the rate of activity, so **statement 1 is correct**.
Adding carbohydrate will have no effect, as the enzyme is already saturated, so **statement 2 is incorrect.**
Adding amylase will increase the amount of carbohydrate that can be converted per unit time, thus increasing the rate, so **statement 3 is correct**.
Increasing the temperature to 100° C will denature the enzyme and reduce the rate, so **statement 4 is incorrect.**

Question 61: E
Taking the healthy allele to be C and the disease conferring allele to be c, this Punnet square models the potential offspring:

		Carrier Mother	
		C	c
Diseased Father	c	Cc	cc
	c	Cc	cc

The gender of the children is irrelevant as the inheritance is autosomal recessive, but we see that all children produced would inherit at least one disease-conferring allele (c).

TOUGH GCSE WORKBOOK: SCIENCE — ANSWERS

Question 62: F
All of the organs listed have endocrine functions.
The thyroid produces thyroid hormone.
The ovary produces oestrogen.
The pancreas secretes glucagon and insulin.
The testes produce testosterone.

Question 63: A
Insulin works to decrease blood glucose levels. Glucagon causes blood glucose levels to increase; glycogen is a carbohydrate. Adrenaline works to increase heart rate.

Question 64: A
The left side of the heart contains oxygenated blood from the lungs which will be pumped to the body. The right side of the heart contains deoxygenated blood from the body to be pumped to the lungs.

Question 65: A
Since Individual 1 is homozygous and healthy, and individual 5 is heterozygous and affected, the disease must be dominant. Since males only have one X-chromosome, they cannot be carriers for X-linked conditions. If Nafram syndrome was X-linked, then parents 5 and 6 would produce sons who always have no disease and daughters that always do. As this is not the case shown in individuals 7-10, the disease must be **autosomal dominant**.

Question 66: C

We know that the inheritance of Nafram syndrome is autosomal dominant, so using N to mean a disease conferring allele and n to mean a healthy allele, 5, 7 and 8 must be Nn because they have an unaffected parent. 2 is also Nn, as if it was NN all its progeny would be Nn and so affected by the disease, which is not the case, as 3 and 4 are unaffected.

Question 67: A

Since 6 is disease free, his genotype must be nn. Thus, neither of 6's parents could be NN, as otherwise 6 would have at least one diseased allele.

Question 68: A

Urine passes from the kidney into the ureter and is then stored in the bladder. It is finally released through the urethra.

Question 69: E

Deoxygenated blood from the body flows through the **inferior vena cava** to the **right atrium**. From the RA, it flows to the **right ventricle** to be pumped via the **pulmonary artery** to the **lungs,** where it is **oxygenated**.

Oxygenated blood then returns to the heart via the **pulmonary vein** into the **left atrium,** then into the **left ventricle**, where it is pumped to the body via the **aorta.**

Correct passage of blood: Left Atrium → Left Ventricle → Aorta → Inferior Vena Cava → Right Atrium → Right Ventricle → Pulmonary Artery → Lungs → Pulmonary Vein → Left Atrium...

Question 70: E
During inspiration, the pressure in the lungs decreases as the diaphragm contracts, increasing the volume of the lungs. The intercostal muscles contract in inspiration, lifting the rib cage up and out to increase intrathoracic volume.

Question 71: D
Whilst **A**, **B**, **C** and **E** are true of the DNA code, they do not represent the property described, which is that more than one combination of codons can encode the same amino acid, e.g. Serine is coded by the sequences: TCT, TCC, TCA, TCG.

Question 72: B
The degenerate nature of the code can help to reduce the deleterious effects of point mutations. The several 3-nucleotide combinations (triplets) that code for each amino acid are usually similar such that a point mutation, i.e. a substitution of one nucleotide for another, can still result in the same amino acid as the one coded for by the original sequence. The degenerate nature of the code does little to protect against deletions/insertions/duplications, which will cause the bases to be read in incorrect triplets, i.e. result in a frame shift.

Question 73: D
The hypothalamus is the site of central thermoreceptors.
A decrease in environmental temperature decreases sweat secretion and causes vasoconstriction of the blood vessels near the skin, to minimise heat loss from the blood.

TOUGH GCSE WORKBOOK: SCIENCE — ANSWERS

Question 74: A
The movement of carbon dioxide in the lungs and neurotransmitters in a synapse are both examples of diffusion. Glucose reabsorption is an active process, as it requires work to be done against a concentration gradient.

Question 75: E
Some enzymes contain other molecules besides protein, e.g. metal ions. Enzymes can increase rates of reaction that may result in heat gain/loss, depending on if the reaction is exothermic or endothermic. They are highly sensitive to variations in pH and their chemical structure is extremely specific to their individual substrate.

CHEMISTRY ANSWERS

Question 76: D
Different isotopes are differentiated by the number of neutrons in the core. This gives them different molecular weights and different chemical properties with regards to stability. The number of protons defines each element, and the number of electrons determine its overall charge.

Question 77: E
A displacement reaction occurs when a more reactive element displaces a less reactive element in its compound. All 4 reactions are examples of displacement reactions as a less reactive element is being replaced by a more reactive one.

Question 78: A
There needs to be 3Ca, 12H, 14O and 2P on each side. Only option **A** satisfies this.

Question 79: A
To balance the equation there needs to be 9Ag, 9N, $9O_3$, 9K, 3P on each side. Only option **A** satisfies this.

Question 80: D
A more reactive halogen can displace a less reactive halogen. Thus, chlorine can displace bromine and iodine from an aqueous solution of its salts, and fluorine can replace chlorine. The trend is the opposite for alkali metals, where reactivity increases down the group as electrons are further from the core and easier to lose.

Question 81: C
$2Mg + O_2 = 2MgO$. So, $2 \times 24 = 48$ and $2 \times (24 + 16) = 80$. So, 48 g of magnesium produces 80g of magnesium oxide. So 1g of magnesium produces 1g × 80g/48g = 1.666g oxide. So 75g × 1.666 = 125g

Question 82: B
$H_2 + 2OH^- \rightarrow 2H_2O + e^-$
Thus, the hydrogen loses electrons i.e. is oxidised.

Question 83: E
1 – correct – this is the formula of ammonia.
2 – correct – ammonia is 1 nitrogen and 3 hydrogen atoms bonded covalently. N = 14g and H = 1g per mole, so percentage of N in NH_3 = 14g/17g = 82%.
3 – correct – it can be broken down to nitrogen and hydrogen, through decomposition.
4 – correct – the bonds between N and H are covalent.
5 – correct – ammonia is an important ingredient in fertilisers.
All of the statements are correct, thus the answer is **E**.

Question 84: A
Whole milk has a roughly neutral pH (~7.0) and contains **fat**. This is broken down by **lipase** to form **fatty acids** - turning the solution slightly more acidic.

Question 85: C
Glucose loses four hydrogen atoms; one definition of an oxidation reaction is a reaction in which there is loss of hydrogen.

Question 86: C
Isotopes have the same number of protons and electrons, but a different number of neutrons. The number of neutrons has no impact on the rate of reactions or on the overall charge of the isotope.

Question 87: E

$Mg + H_2SO_4 \rightarrow MgSO_4 + H_2$

Number of moles of Mg = $\frac{6}{24}$ = 0.25 moles.

1 mole of Mg reacts with 1 mole H_2SO_4 to produce 1 mole of magnesium sulphate. Therefore, 0.25 moles H_2SO_4 will react to produce 0.25 moles of $MgSO_4$.

M_r of H_2SO_4 = 2 + 32 + 64 = 98g per mole

The mass of H_2SO_4 used = 0.25 moles × 98g per mole = 24.5g.

Since 30g of H_2SO_4 is present, H_2SO_4 is in excess and the magnesium is the limiting reagent.

M_r of $MgSO_4$ = 24 + 32 + 64 = 120g per mole

The mass of $MgSO_4$ produced = 0.25 moles × 120g per mole = 30g which is the same mass as that of sulphuric acid in the original reaction.

Question 88: E

Reactivity series of metals:

Cu is more reactive than Ag and will displace it.

Ca is more reactive than H and will displace it.

2 and 4 are incorrect because Fe is higher in the reactivity series than Cu and Fe is lower in the reactivity series than Ca, so no displacement will occur.

Question 89: E

1 – incorrect – moving left to right is the equivalent of moving down the metal reactivity series (i.e. Na is most reactive and Zn is least reactive). Therefore, moving from left to right, the reactivity of the metals **decreases**.

2 – incorrect – moving L to R, the reactivity decreases so the likelihood of corrosion of the metals decreases, rather than **increases**.

3 – incorrect – moving L to R, the reactivity decreases, so **less** energy is required to separate metals from their ores.

4 – incorrect – moving L to R, the reactivity decreases, so metals lose electrons **less** readily to form positive ions.

None of the statements given are correct, thus the answer is **E**.

Question 90: E

Halogens become less reactive as you progress down group 17. Thus, in order of increasing reactivity from left to right: I→ Br→ Cl. Therefore, I will not displace Br, Cl will displace Br and Br will displace I.

Question 91: A

Wires are made out of copper because it is a good conductor of electricity. Copper is also used in coins (not aluminium). Aluminium is resistant to corrosion but because of a layer of aluminium oxide (not hydroxide).

Question 92: C

2Li + 2H$_2$O → 2LiOH + H$_2$

Therefore, 2 moles of Li react to produce 1 mole of H$_2$ gas (24 dm^3).

The number of moles of Li = $\frac{21}{7}$ = 3 moles.

Thus, 1.5 moles of H$_2$ gas are produced = 36 dm^3.

Question 93: B

MgCl$_2$ contains stronger bonds than NaCl because Mg ions have a 2+ charge, thus having a stronger electrostatic pull for negative chloride ions. The smaller atomic radius also means that the nucleus has less distance between it and incoming electrons. Transition metals are able to form multiple stable ions e.g. Fe^{2+} and Fe^{3+}. Covalently bonded structures do tend to have lower melting points than ionically bonded, but the giant covalent structures (diamond and graphite for example) have very high melting points. Graphite is an example of a covalently bonded structure which conducts electricity.

Question 94: D

Energy is released from reaction **A**, as shown by a negative enthalpy. The reaction is therefore exothermic. Since energy is released, the product CO$_2$ has less energy than the reactants did. Therefore, CO$_2$ is more stable. Reaction **B** has a positive enthalpy, which means energy must be put into the reaction for it to occur i.e. it's an endothermic reaction. That means that the products (CaO and CO$_2$) have more energy and are less stable than the reactants (CaCO$_3$).

TOUGH GCSE WORKBOOK: SCIENCE — ANSWERS

Question 95: B
Solid oxides are unable to conduct electricity because the ions are immobile. Metals are extracted from their molten ores by electrolysis. Fractional distillation is used to separate miscible liquids with similar boiling points. Mg^{2+} ions have a greater positive charge and a smaller ionic radius than Na^+ ions, and therefore have stronger bonds.

Question 96: E
Li^+ (2) and Na^+ (2, 8)
Mg^{2+} (2, 8) and Ne (2, 8)
Na^{2+} (2, 7) and Ne (2, 8)
O^{2+} (2, 4) and a Carbon atom (2, 4)

Question 97: B
Reactivity of both group 1 and 2 increases as you go down the groups because the valence electrons that react are further away from the positively charged nucleus (which means the electrostatic attraction between them is weaker). Group 1 metals are usually more reactive because they only need to donate one electron, whilst group 2 metals must donate two electrons.

Question 98: D
This is a straightforward question that tests basic understanding of kinetics. Catalysts help overcome energy barriers by reducing the activation energy necessary for a reaction.

Question 99: D
H^1 contains 1 proton and no neutrons. Isotopes have the same numbers of protons, but different numbers of neutrons. Thus, H^3 contains two more neutrons than H^1.

Question 100: D
Oxidation is the loss of electrons and reduction is the gain of electrons (therefore increasing electron density). Halogens tend to act as electron recipients in reactions and are therefore good oxidising agents.

Question 101: D
These statements all come from the Kinetic Theory of Gases, an idealised model of gases that allows for the derivation of the ideal gas law. The angle at which gas molecules move is not related to temperature; movement is random. Gas molecules lose no energy when they collide with each other. Collisions are assumed to be elastic. The average kinetic energy of gas molecules is the same for all gases at the same temperature as they are assumed to be point masses. Momentum = mass x velocity. Therefore, the momentum of gas molecules increases with pressure as a greater force is exerted on each molecule.

Question 102: E
An exothermic reaction is defined as a chemical reaction that releases energy. Thus, aerobic respiration, the burning of magnesium, and the reacting of acids/bases are almost always exothermic processes. Similarly, the combustion of most things (including hydrogen) is exothermic. Evaporation of water is a physical process in which no chemical reaction is taking place.

Question 103: E

$2 C_3H_6 + 9 O_2 \rightarrow 6 H_2O + 6 CO_2$

Assign the oxidation numbers for each element:
For C_3H_6: C = -2; H = +1
For O_2: O = 0
For H_2O: H = +1; O = -2
For CO_2: C = +4; O = -2
Look for the changes in the oxidation numbers:
H remained at +1
C changed from -2 to +4. Thus, it was oxidized
O changed from 0 to -2. Thus, it was reduced.

Question 104: B

The equation for the reaction is: $Zn + CuSO_4 \rightarrow ZnSO_4 + Cu$
Assign oxidation numbers for each element:
For Zn: Zn = 0
For $CuSO_4$: Cu = +2; S = +6; O = -2
For $ZnSO_4$: Zn = +2; S = +6; O = -2
For Cu: Cu = 0
With these oxidation numbers, we can see that Zn was oxidized and Cu in $CuSO_4$ was reduced. Thus, Zn acted as the reducing agent and Cu in $CuSO_4$ is the oxidizing agent.

Question 105: B

Acids are proton donors which only exist in aqueous solution - a liquid state. Strong acids are fully ionised in solution and the reaction between an acid and a base $\rightarrow$ salt + water.
The pH of weak acids is usually between 4 and 6.

TOUGH GCSE WORKBOOK: SCIENCE — ANSWERS

Question 106: D

Let x be the relative abundance of Z^6 and y the relative abundance of Z^8.

The average atomic mass takes the abundances of all 3 isotopes into account.

Thus, (Abundance of Z^5)(Mass Z^5) + (Abundance of Z^6)(Mass Z^6) + (Abundance of Z^8)(Mass Z^8) = 7

Therefore: $(5 \times 0.2) + 6x + 8y = 7$

So: $6x + 8y = 6$

Divide by two to give: $3x + 4y = 3$

The abundances of all isotopes = 100% = 1

This gives: $0.2 + x + y = 1$

Solve the two equations simultaneously:

$y = 0.8 - x \rightarrow 3x + 4(0.8 - x) = 3 \rightarrow 3x + 3.2 - 4x = 3$

Therefore, $x = 0.2$

$y = 0.8 - 0.2 = 0.6$

Thus, the overall abundances are $Z^5 = 20\%$, $Z^6 = 20\%$ and $Z^8 = 60\%$. Therefore, all the statements are correct.

Question 107: A

If a metal is more reactive than hydrogen, a displacement reaction will occur resulting in the formation of a salt made up of the metal cation and hydrogen.

Question 108: B

$6 FeSO_4 + K_2Cr_2O_7 + 7 H_2SO_4 \rightarrow 3 (Fe)_2(SO_4)_3 + Cr_2(SO_4)_3 + K_2SO_4 + 7 H_2O$

In order to save time, you have to quickly eliminate options (rather than try every combination out).

The quickest way is to do this is algebraically:

For Potassium:
$2b = 2e = 2f$
Therefore, $b = f$.
Option **F** does not fulfil $b = e = f$.

For Iron:
$a = 2d$
Options **C**, **D** and **E** don't fulfil $a = 2d$.

For Hydrogen:
$2c = 2g$
Therefore, $c = g$. Option **A** does not fulfil $c = g$. This leaves option **B** as the answer.

Question 109: E

Atoms are electrically neutral. Ions have different numbers of electrons when compared to atoms of the same element. Protons provide just under 50% of an atom's mass; the other 50% is provided by neutrons, with a minimal contribution from the electrons. Isotopes don't exhibit significantly different kinetics. Protons do indeed repel each other in the nucleus (which is one reason why neutrons are needed: to reduce the electrical charge density).

TOUGH GCSE WORKBOOK: SCIENCE — ANSWERS

Question 110: B
The noble gases are extremely useful, e.g. helium in blimps, neon signs, argon in bulbs. They are colourless and odourless and have no valence electrons. As with the rest of the periodic table, boiling point increases as you progress down the group. Helium is the most abundant noble gas (and indeed the 2nd most abundant element in the universe).

Question 111: D
1 – correct – all alkenes contain at least one double bond.
2 – correct – they can be reduced to alkanes.
3 – incorrect – it is an example of a hydrogenation or reduction reaction, not a hydration reaction.
Thus, the answer is **D**.

Question 112: A
The average atomic mass takes the relative abundance of both isotopes into account:
(Abundance of Cl^{35})(Mass Cl^{35}) + (Abundance of Cl^{37})(Mass Cl^{37}) = 35.453
34.969(Abundance of Cl^{35}) + 36.966(Abundance of Cl^{37}) = 35.453
The abundances of both isotopes = 100% = 1
I.e. abundance of Cl^{35} + abundance of Cl^{37} = 1
Therefore: $x + y = 1$ which can be rearranged to give: $y = 1-x$
Therefore: $x + (1 - x) = 1$.
$34.969x + 36.966(1-x) = 35.453$
$x = 0.758$
$1 - x = 0.242$
Therefore, Cl^{35} is 3 times more abundant than Cl^{37}.
Note you could approximate the values here to arrive at the solution quicker, e.g. 34.969 → 35, 36.966 → 37 and 35.453 → 35.5

TOUGH GCSE WORKBOOK: SCIENCE — ANSWERS

Question 113: A
A – correct - transition metals form multiple stable ions, which may have many different colours (e.g. green Fe^{2+} and brown Fe^{3+}).
B – incorrect – transition metals usually for ionic bonds, not covalent.
C – incorrect – transition metals are commonly used as catalysts, e.g. iron in the Haber process.
D – incorrect – transition metals are excellent conductors of electricity.
E – incorrect – transition metals are known as the d-block elements of the periodic table, the alkali earth metals are found in group 2.

Question 114: B
$2Na + 2H_2O \rightarrow 2NaOH + H_2$
8000 $cm^3 = 8$ $dm^3 = ⅓$ moles of H_2
2 moles of Na react completely to form 1 mole of H_2.
Therefore, ⅔ moles of Na must have reacted to produce ⅓ moles of hydrogen. ⅔ x 23g per mole = 15.3g.
% Purity of sample = $\frac{15.3}{20}$ x 100 = 76.5%

TOUGH GCSE WORKBOOK: SCIENCE — ANSWERS

Question 115: C

Assume total mass of molecule is 100g. Therefore, it contains 70.6g carbon, 5.9g hydrogen and 23.5g oxygen. Now, calculate the number of moles of each element using $Moles = \frac{Mass}{Molar\ Mass}$

$Moles\ of\ Carbon = \frac{70.6}{12} \approx 6 \quad Moles\ of\ Hydrogen = \frac{5.9}{1} \approx 6 \quad Moles\ of\ Oxygen = \frac{23.5}{16} \approx 1.5$

Therefore, the molar ratios give an empirical formula of $C_6H_6O_{1.5} = C_4H_4O$.
Molar mass of the empirical formula = (4 × 12) + (4 × 1) + 16 = 68.
Molar mass of chemical formula = 136. Therefore, the chemical formula = $C_8H_8O_2$.

Question 116: B

$S + 6\ HNO_3 \rightarrow H_2SO_4 + 6\ NO_2 + 2\ H_2O$

In order to save time, you have to quickly eliminate options (rather than try every combination out).
The quickest way to do this is algebraically:
For Hydrogen:
$b = 2c + 2e$
Options **A, C, D, E** and **F** don't fulfil $b = 2c + 2e$.
This leaves option **B** as the only possible answer.
Note how quickly we were able to get the correct answer here by choosing an element that appears in 3 molecules (as opposed to Sulphur or Nitrogen which only appear in 2).

Question 117: A
Alkenes undergo addition reactions, such as that with hydrogen, when catalysed by nickel, whilst alkanes do not as they are already fully saturated. The C=C bond is stronger than the C-C bond, but it is not exactly twice as strong, so will not require twice the energy to break it. Both molecules are organic and will dissolve in organic solvents.

Question 118: E
Diamond is unable to conduct electricity because all the electrons are involved in covalent bonds. Graphite is insoluble in water and organic solvents. Graphite is also able to conduct electricity because it has free electrons that are not involved in covalent bonds. Methane and ammonia both have low melting points. Methane is not a polar molecule, so cannot conduct electricity or dissolve in water. Ammonia is polar and will dissolve in water. It can conduct electricity in aqueous form, but not as a gas.

Question 119: A
Catalysts increase the rate of reaction by providing an alternative route for reaction with a lower activation energy, which means that less energy is required and as a result, costs are reduced. The point of equilibrium, the nature of the products, and the overall energy change are unaffected by catalysts.

Question 120: E
The 5 carbon atoms in this hydrocarbon make it a "pent" stem. The C=C bond makes it an alkene, and the location of this bond is the 2nd position, making the molecule pent-2-ene.

Question 121: D
Group 1 elements form positively charged ions in most reactions since they lose electrons. Thus, the oxidation number must increase. Their reactivity increases as the valence electrons are further away from the positively charged nucleus down group. All group one elements react spontaneously with oxygen – the less reactive ones form an oxide coating and the more reactive ones spontaneously burn.

Question 122: E
The cathode attracts positively charged ions. The cathode reduces ions and the anode oxidises ions. Electrolysis can be used to separate compounds but not mixtures (i.e. substances that are not chemically joined).

Question 123: B
Pentane, C_5H_{12}, has a total of 3 isomers. **A, C** and **D** are correctly configured. However, the 4th Carbon atom in option **B** has more than 4 bonds which wouldn't be possible. If you're stuck on this – draw them out!

Question 124: E
$3\ Cu + 8\ HNO_3 \rightarrow 3\ Cu(NO_3)_2 + 2\ NO + 4\ H_2O$
In order to save time, you have to quickly eliminate options (rather than try every combination out). The quickest way to do this is algebraically, by first assigning coefficients to the equation: $aCu + bHNO_3 \rightarrow cCu(NO_3)_2 + dNO + eH_2O$. For Nitrogen: $b = 2c + d$. In this case, only option **E** satisfies $b = 2c + d$.
Note that using copper wouldn't be as useful, as all the options satisfy $a = c$.

TOUGH GCSE WORKBOOK: SCIENCE — ANSWERS

Question 125: D
Alkenes are an organic series and have twice as many hydrogen atoms as carbon atoms. Bromine water is decolourised in their presence, and they take part in addition reactions. Alkenes are more reactive than alkanes because they contain a C=C bond.

Question 126: A
A – correct – group 17 elements are missing one valence electron, so form negative ions.
B – incorrect – reactivity decreases as you progress down group 17, so fluorine reacts **more** vigorously than iodine.
C – incorrect – all group 17 elements are found bound to each other e.g. F_2 and Cl_2.

Question 127: D
CO poisoning and spontaneous combustion do not occur in the electrolysis of brine. The products of cathode and anode in the electrolysis of brine are Cl_2 and H_2. If these two gases react with each other they can form HCl, which is extremely corrosive.

Question 128: D
The hydrogen produced is positively charged and therefore needs to be reduced by the addition of an electron before being released. This happens at the cathode. The chlorine produced is negatively charged and therefore needs to lose electrons. This happens at the anode. NaOH is formed in this process.

Question 129: C
Alkanes are made of chains of singly bonded carbon and hydrogen atoms. C-H bonds are very strong and confer alkanes a great deal of stability. An alkane with 14 hydrogen atoms is called hexane, as it has 6 carbon atoms. Alkanes burn in excess oxygen to produce carbon dioxide and water. Bromine water is decolourised in the presence of alkenes.

Question 130: E
Alcohols by definition contain an R-OH functional group and because of this polar group are highly soluble in water. Ethanol is a common biofuel.

Question 131: E
Alkanes are saturated (and therefore non-reducible), have the general formula C_nH_{2n+2} and have no effect on Bromine solution. Alkenes are unsaturated (and therefore reducible), have the general formula C_nH_{2n} and turn bromine water colourless because they can undergo an addition reaction with bromine.

Question 132: D
The balanced equation for the reaction between magnesium oxide and hydrochloric acid is:
$MgO + 2HCl \rightarrow MgCl_2 + H_2$
The relative molecular mass of MgO is 24 + 16 = 40g per mole.
Therefore, 10g of MgO represents 10/40 = 0.25 moles.
As the ratio of MgO to $MgCl_2$ is 1:1, we know that the amount of $MgCl_2$ produced will also be 0.25 moles. One mole of $MgCl_2$ has a molecular mass of 24 + (2 × 35.5) = 95g per mole.
Therefore, the reaction will produce 0.25 × 95 = 23.75g of $MgCl_2$.

TOUGH GCSE WORKBOOK: SCIENCE — ANSWERS

Question 133: D
Moving up the alkane series, as the size and mass of the molecule increases, the boiling point and viscosity increase, and the flammability and volatility decrease. Pentadecane will be more viscous than pentane.

Question 134: E
All of the factors mentioned will affect the rate of a reaction.
The temperature affects the movement rate of particles, which if moving faster in higher temperatures will collide more often, thus increasing the rate of reaction.
Collision rate is also increased with a higher **concentration** of reactants, and with a higher concentration of a **catalyst** or one with larger **surface area**, which will provide more active sites, thus increasing the rate of reaction.

Question 135: C
The total atomic mass of the end product is $C[12 + (2 \times 16)] + D[(2 \times 1) + 16] = 44C + 18D$
We know that $176 = 44C$. Therefore $C = 4$, and that $108 = 18D$ so $D = 6$.
Thus, the equation becomes: $C_aH_b + O_2 \rightarrow 4CO_2 + 6H_2O$.
This gives a ratio of 4C to 12H, which is a ratio of 1:3 carbon to hydrogen. This means the unknown hydrocarbon must be a multiple of this ratio. By balancing the equation, we can see that the unknown hydrocarbon must be ethane, C_2H_6: $2C_2H_6 + 7O_2 \rightarrow 4CO_2 + 6H_2O$.

Question 136: A
$C_2H_5OH \rightarrow C_2H_4O$. Thus, ethanol has lost two hydrogen atoms, i.e. it has been oxidised. Note that although another substrate may be reduced (therefore making it a redox reaction), ethanol itself has only been oxidised.

Question 137: B
This is fairly straightforward, but you can save time by doing it algebraically:
For barium: $3a = b$. For nitrogen: $2a = c$. Let $a = 1$, thus, $b = 3$ and $c = 2$

Question 138: E
There are 14 oxygen atoms on the left side. Thus: $3b + 2c = 14$.
Note also that for sulfur: $a = c$, and for Iron: $a = 2b$.
This sets up an easy trio of simultaneous equations:
Substitute a into the first equation to give: $1.5a + 2a = 14$. Thus: $a = 14/3.5 = 4$.
Therefore, $a = c = 4$ and $b = 2$

Question 139: C
The average atomic mass takes the relative abundance of all isotopes found in nature into account:
Mass = (Abundance of Mg^{23})(Mass Mg^{23}) + (Abundance of Mg^{25})(Mass Mg^{25}) + (Abundance of Mg^{26})(Mass Mg^{26})
$Mass = 23 \times 0.80 + 25 \times 0.10 + 26 \times 0.10$
$= 18.4 + 2.5 + 2.6 = 23.5$

Question 140: D

Cl_2 and Fe_2O_3 are reduced in their reactions and are therefore oxidising agents. Similarly, CO and Cu^{2+} are oxidised in their reactions and are therefore reducing agents. Cl is a stronger oxidising agent than Br as it is higher up in the reactivity series and will displace negative Br ions from its compounds to form the oxidised Br_2. Mg is a stronger reducing agent than Cu, as it is higher up in the reactivity series. Thus, Mg would displace a positive copper ion from its compound to form copper atoms. Therefore, Mg reduces Cu.

Question 141: C

NaCl is an ionic compound and therefore has a high melting point. It is highly soluble in water but only conducts electricity in solution/as a liquid.

Question 142: C

The equation for the reaction is: $2NaOH + Zn(NO_3)_2 \rightarrow 2NaNO_3 + Zn(OH)_2$

Therefore, the molar ratio between NaOH and $Zn(OH)_2$ is 2:1.
Molecular Mass of NaOH = 23 + 16 + 1 = 40
Molecular Mass of $Zn(OH)_2$ = 65 + 17 x 2 = 99
Thus, the number of moles of NaOH that react = 80/40 = 2 moles. Therefore, 1 mole of $Zn(OH)_2$ is produced. Mass = 99g per mole x 1 mole = 99g

Question 143: E

Metal + Water $\rightarrow$ Hydroxide + Hydrogen gas; the reaction is always exothermic. Reactivity increases down the group, so potassium reacts more vigorously with water than sodium. Therefore, all four statements are correct.

TOUGH GCSE WORKBOOK: SCIENCE — ANSWERS

Question 144: C
Electrolysis separates NaCl into sodium and chloride ions but not CO_2 (which is a covalently bound gas). Sieves cannot separate ionically bound compounds like NaCl. Dyes are miscible liquids and can be separated by chromatography. Oil and water are immiscible liquids, so a separating funnel is necessary to separate the mixtures. Methane and diesel are separated from each other during fractional distillation, as they have different boiling points.

Question 145: B
The reaction between water and caesium can cause spontaneous combustion, so it doesn't make the reaction safer. The reaction between caesium and fluoride is highly exothermic and does not require a catalyst. The reaction produces CsF, which is a salt.

Question 146: B
The nuclei of larger elements contain more neutrons than protons which reduces the charge density, e.g. Br^{80} contains 35 protons but 45 neutrons. Stable isotopes very rarely undergo radioactive decay.

Question 147: B
The vast majority of salts contain ionic bonds that require a significant amount of thermal energy to break.

Question 148: E
306ml of water is 306g, which is the equivalent of 306g/18g per mole of H_2O = 17 moles. 17 times Avogadro's constant gives the number of molecules present, which is 1.02×10^{25}. There are 10 protons and 10 electrons in each water molecule. Hence there are 1.02×10^{26} protons.

TOUGH GCSE WORKBOOK: SCIENCE — ANSWERS

Question 149: D
The number of moles of each element = Mass/Molar Mass. Let the % represent the mass in grams: Hydrogen: 3.45g/1g per mole = 3.45 moles. Oxygen: 55.2g/16g per mole = 3.45 moles
Carbon: 41.4g/12g per mole = 3.45 moles
Thus, the molar ratio is 1:1:1. The only option that satisfies this is option **D**.

Question 150: C
Group 17 elements are non-metals, whilst group 2 elements are metals. Thus, the Group 17 element must gain electrons when it reacts with the Group 2 element, i.e. B is reduced. The easy way to calculate the formula is to swap the valences of both elements: A is +2 and B is -1. Thus, the compound is AB_2.

PHYSICS ANSWERS

Question 151: E
The amplitude of a wave does not determine the mass of the wave. Waves are not objects and thus do not have mass.

A – correct – microwaves are an example of using electromagnetic waves to heat things up!
B – correct – these waves have high energy and thus can knock electrons out of their orbits.
C – correct.
D – correct – this is a 'green' method of producing electricity.

TOUGH GCSE WORKBOOK: SCIENCE ANSWERS

Question 152: A
We know that displacement s = 30 m, initial speed u = 0 ms⁻¹, acceleration a = 5.4 ms⁻², final speed v = ?, time t = ?
And that $v^2 = u^2 + 2as$
$v^2 = 0 + 2 \times 5.4 \times 30$
$v^2 = 324$ so v = 18 ms⁻¹
and s = ut + 1/2 at² so 30 = 1/2 x 5.4 x t²
To find 30/2.7 without a calculator, find a rough estimate by substituting 2.7 for 3, to give 30/3 = 10.
We now know that t^2 will be a shade over 10, as the actual number we should be dividing by (2.7) was smaller than the number we used in the estimate.
If t^2 is just over 10, we can exclude t = 3.1 as an option, as 3.1^2 is 9.61 i.e. under 10, rather than over.
The only option that remains that gives $v = 18 \text{ms}^{-1}$ is option A, which gives 3.3 as an answer for t.
We can quickly calculate that 3.3^2 would give us 10.89 for t, which is a shade over 10 – i.e. exactly what we are looking for!

Question 153: D
Consider the following equations:
- Velocity = λf
- Frequency = 1/T
- These 2 equations can be combined and rearranged to give λ = vT

The period T of one wave = $\frac{49s}{7}$ = 7s, so λ = 5 ms⁻¹ x 7 s = 35 m.

Question 154: E

This is a straightforward question as you only have to put the numbers into the equation (made harder by the numbers being hard to work with).

$$Power = \frac{Force \times Distance}{Time}$$

$Force = mass \times acceleration = 37.5 \times 10$

$$\frac{375\,N \times 1.3\,m}{5\,s}$$

We can simplify 375/5 to 75, thus making the calculation easier.
$= 75 \times 1.3 = 97.5\,W$

Question 155: E

$v = u + at$
$v = 0 + 5.6 \times 8 = 44.8$ ms^{-1}

And $s = ut + \frac{at^2}{2} = 0 + 5.6 \times \frac{8^2}{2} = 179.2$

Question 156: C

The skydiver leaves the plane and will accelerate until the air resistance equals their weight – this is their terminal velocity. The skydiver will accelerate under the force of gravity. If the air resistance force exceeded the force of gravity the skydiver would accelerate away from the ground, and if it was less than the force of gravity they would continue to accelerate toward the ground.

TOUGH GCSE WORKBOOK: SCIENCE — ANSWERS

Question 157: D
s = 20 m, u = 0 ms^{-1}, a = 10 ms^{-2}
and v^2 = u^2 + 2as
v^2 = 0 + 2 × 10 × 20
v^2 = 400; v = 20 ms^{-1}
Momentum = Mass x velocity = 20 x 0.1 = 2 kgms^{-1}

Question 158: E
Electromagnetic waves have varying wavelengths and frequencies and their energy is proportional to their frequency – hence options 3 and 4 are incorrect.
Unlike sound waves, EM waves can all travel through a vacuum and can be reflected – hence options 1 and 2 are correct.

Question 159: D
The total resistance in a series circuit can be found by adding the individual resistances – this is a 'series' circuit as the battery (resistance 0.8) and the drill (resistance 1) are in series.
Total resistance = R + r = 0.8 + 1 = 1.8 Ω
and $I = \dfrac{e.m.f}{total\ resistance} = \dfrac{36}{1.8} = 20\ A$

Question 160: D
Use Newton's second law → $F = ma$
Remember to work in SI units!
So $Force = mass \times accelaration = mass \times \dfrac{\Delta velocity}{time}$
$= 20 \times 10^{-3} \times \dfrac{100 - 0}{10 \times 10^{-3}}$
$= 200\ N$

TOUGH GCSE WORKBOOK: SCIENCE — ANSWERS

Question 161: E
In this case, the work being done is moving the bag 0.7 m
i.e. $Work\ Done = Bag's\ Weight \times Distance = 50 \times 10 \times 0.7 = 350\ N$
$Power = \dfrac{Work}{Time} = \dfrac{350}{3} = 116.7\ W$
= 117 W to 3 significant figures

Question 162: B
Firstly, use P = Fv to calculate the power [Ignore the frictional force as we are not concerned with the resultant force here].
So P = 300 × 30 = 9000 W
Then, use P = IV to calculate the current.
I = P/V = 9000/200 = 45 A

Question 163: C
Work is defined as W = F × s. Work can also be defined as work = force × distance moved in the direction of force. Work is measured in joules and 1 Joule = 1 Newton × 1 Metre, and 1 Newton = 1 Kg × ms^{-2} [F = ma].
Thus, 1 Joule = Kgm^{2}s^{-2}

Question 164: E
Joules are the unit of energy (and also Work = Force × Distance).
Thus, 1 Joule = 1 N × 1 m.
Pa is the unit of Pressure (= Force/Area). Thus, Pa = N × m^{-2}. So J = Nm^{-2} × m^3 = Pa × m^3. Newton's third law describes that every action produces an equal and opposite reaction. For this reason, the energy required to decelerate a body is equal to the amount of energy it possesses during movement, i.e. its kinetic energy, which is defined as in statement 1.

Question 165: D
Alpha radiation is of the lowest energy, as it represents the movement of a fairly large particle consisting of 2 neutrons and 2 protons. Beta radiation consists of high-energy, high-speed electrons or positrons.

Question 166: E
The half-life does depend on atom type and isotope, as these parameters significantly impact on the physical properties of the atom in general, so statement 1 is false. Statement 2 is the correct definition of half-life. Statement 3 is also correct: half-life in exponential decay will always have the same duration, independent of the quantity of the matter in question; in non-exponential decay, half-life is dependent on the quantity of matter in question.

Question 167: C
192 / 24 = 8 half-lives have elapsed. So, we can calculate: $56 \times 2^8 = 14,336$ = the original count rate.

Question 168: A
1 – correct – the rate of decay decreases exponentially as the material decays.
2 – incorrect – remember, not all nuclei of the same element are the same, as the number of neutrons can be different. Nuclei with different numbers of neutrons will have different half-lives. However, all nuclei of the same *isotope* of an element will have the same half-life.
3 – incorrect – radioactive decay is a highly unpredictable process.

TOUGH GCSE WORKBOOK: SCIENCE — ANSWERS

Question 169: E
The total resistance of the circuit would be twice the resistance of one resistor and proportional to the voltage, as given by Ohm's Law. Since it is a series circuit, the same current flows through each resistor and since they are identical the potential difference across each resistor will be the same.

Question 170: E
The distance between Earth and Sun = Time x Speed = 60 x 8 seconds x 3×10^8 ms^{-1} = $480 \times 3 \times 10^8$ m
Approximately = 1500×10^8 = 1.5×10^{11} m.
The circumference of Earth's orbit around the sun is given by $2\pi r$
= $2 \times 3 \times 1.5 \times 10^{11}$
= 9×10^{11} = 10^{12} m

Question 171: E
Speed is a scalar quantity whilst velocity is a vector describing both magnitude and direction. Speed describes the distance a moving object covers over time (i.e. speed = distance/time), whereas velocity describes the rate of change of the displacement of an object (i.e. velocity = displacement/time). The international standardised unit for speed is meters per second (ms^{-1}), while ms^{-2} is the unit of acceleration.

Question 172: E
Ohm's Law only applies to conductors and can be mathematically expressed as $V \alpha I$. The easiest way to do this is to write down the equations for statements c, d and e. **C**: $I \alpha \frac{1}{V}$; **D**: $I \alpha V^2$; **E**: $I \alpha V$. Thus, statement **E** is correct.

Question 173: E

Any object at rest is not accelerating and therefore has no resultant force. Strictly speaking, Newton's second law is actually: Force = rate of change of momentum, which can be mathematically manipulated to give statement 2:

$$Force = \frac{momentum}{time} = \frac{mass \times velocity}{time} = mass \times accelaration$$

Thus, all of the statements are correct.

Question 174: D

Statement 3 is incorrect, as $Charge = Current \times time$. Statement 1 substitutes $I = \frac{V}{R}$ and statement 2 substitutes $I = \frac{P}{V}$.

Question 175: E

Applying Newton's second law of motion gives:
Weight of elevator + people = mg = 10 × (1600 + 200) = 18,000 N
Thus, the resultant force is given by:
F_M = Motor Force − [Frictional Force + Weight]
F_M = M − 4,000 − 18,000
Use Newton's second law to give: F_M = M − 22,000 N = ma
Thus, M − 22,000 N = 1,800a
Since the lift must accelerate at 1ms^{-2}: M = 1,800 kg × 1 ms^{-2} + 22,000 N
M = 23,800 N

Question 176: D

Total Distance = Distance during acceleration phase + Distance during braking phase

Distance during the acceleration phase is given by:

$$s = ut + \frac{at^2}{2} = 0 + \frac{5 \times 10^2}{2} = 250\ m$$

$$v = u + at = 0 + 5 \times 10 = 50\ ms^{-1}$$

And use $a = \frac{v-u}{t}$ to calculate the deceleration: $a = \frac{0-50}{20} = -2.5\ ms^{-2}$

Distance during the deceleration phase is given by:

$$s = ut + \frac{at^2}{2} = 50 \times 20 + \frac{-2.5 \times 20^2}{2} = 1000 - \frac{2.5 \times 400}{2}$$

$$s = 1000 - 500 = 500\ m$$

Thus, $Total\ Distance = 250 + 500 = 750\ m$

Question 177: E

It is not possible to calculate the power of the heater as we don't know the current that flows through it or its internal resistance. The 8 ohms refers to the external copper wire and not the heater. Whilst it's important that you know how to use equations like P = IV, it's just as important that you know when you **can't** use them!

Question 178: E

This question has a lot of numbers but not any information on time, which is necessary to calculate power. You cannot calculate power by using P= IV as you don't know how many electrons are accelerated through the potential difference per unit time. Thus, more information is required to calculate the power.

Question 179: B

When an object is in equilibrium with its surroundings, it radiates and absorbs energy at the same rate and so its temperature remains constant i.e. there is no *net* energy transfer. Radiation is slower than conduction and convection.

Question 180: A

The work done by the force is given by: $Work\ Done = Force \times Distance = 12\,N \times 3\,m = 36\,J$
Since the surface is frictionless, $Work\ Done = Kinetic\ Energy$.
$E_k = \frac{mv^2}{2} = \frac{6v^2}{2}$
Thus, $36 = 3v^2$
$v = \sqrt{12} = \sqrt{4}\sqrt{3} = 2\sqrt{3}\ ms^{-1}$

Question 181: C

$Total\ energy\ supplied\ to\ water$
$= Change\ in\ temperature \times Mass\ of\ water \times 4,000\,J$
$= 40 \times 1.5 \times 4,000 = 240,000\,J$
$Power\ of\ the\ heater = \frac{Work\ Done}{time} = \frac{240,000}{50 \times 60} = \frac{240,000}{3,000} = 80\,W$. Using $P = IV = \frac{V^2}{R}$:
$R = \frac{V^2}{P} = \frac{100^2}{80} = \frac{10,000}{80} = 125\ ohms$

Question 182: C

1 – incorrect – the half life of a radioactive substance is defined as the time taken for the radioactivity of a specific isotope to fall to half its original value.

2 – correct – a beta particle is essentially a high energy election, that is emitted from the nucleus. Beta emission occurs when a neutron is converted to a proton and an electron, and it occurs in elements which have too many neutrons relative to the number of protons. The element gains a proton in the process of beta emission, so it is converted to a new element.

3 – incorrect – this is true of beta emission, not alpha. An alpha particle is made up of 2 protons and 2 neutrons, the equivalent of a helium nucleus.

Question 183: D

Gravitational potential energy is just an extension of the equation work done = force x distance (force is the weight of the object, mg, and distance is the height, h). The reservoir in statement 3 would have a potential energy of 10^{10} Joules i.e. 10 Giga Joules ($E_p = 10^6$ kg x 10 N x 10^3 m).

Question 184: D

Statement 1 is the common formulation of Newton's third law.
Statement 2 presents a consequence of the application of Newton's third law.
Statement 3 is false: the force of the rifle recoiling will be the same as the force of the bullet going forward, but the acceleration will be different as the masses of each are different ($F = ma$).

Question 185: E
Positively charged objects have lost electrons.
$$Charge = Current \times Time = \frac{Voltage}{Resistance} \times Time.$$
Objects can become charged by friction as electrons are transferred from one object to the other.

Question 186: B
Each body of mass exerts a gravitational force on another body with mass. This is true for all planets as well. Gravitational force is dependent on the mass of both objects. Satellites stay in orbit due to centripetal force that acts tangentially to gravity (not because of the thrust from their engines). Two objects will only land at the same time if they also have the same shape or they are in a vaccum (as otherwise air resistance would result in different terminal velocities).

Question 187: A
Metals conduct electrical charge easily and provide little resistance to the flow of electrons. Charge can also flow in several directions. However, all conductors have an internal resistance and therefore provide *some* resistance to electrical charge.

Question 188: E

First, calculate the rate of petrol consumption:
$$\frac{Speed}{Consumption} = \frac{60 \ miles/hour}{30 \ miles/gallon} = 2 \ gallons/hour$$
Therefore, the total power is:
$2 \ gallons = 2 \times 9 \times 10^8 = 18 \times 10^8 J$
$1 \ hour = 60 \times 60 = 3600 \ s$
Power $= \frac{Energy}{Time} = \frac{18 \times 10^8}{3600} = \frac{18}{36} \times 10^6 = 5 \times 10^5 \ W$
Since efficiency is 20%, the power delivered to the wheels $=$
$5 \times 10^5 \times 0.2 = 10^5 \ W = 100 \ kW$

Question 189: D

Beta radiation is stopped by a few millimetres of aluminium, but not by paper. In β^- radiation, a neutron becomes a proton plus an emitted electron. This means the atomic mass number remains unchanged.

Question 190: E

Firstly, calculate the mass of the car $= \frac{Weight}{g} = \frac{15,000}{10} = 1,500 \ kg$
Then using $v = u + at$ where v = 0 ms^{-1} and u = 15 ms^{-1} and t = 10 × 10^{-3} s
$a = \frac{0-15}{0.01} = 1500 ms^{-2}$
$F = ma = 1500 \times 1500 = 2 \ 250 \ 000 \ N$

Question 191: E
Electrical insulators offer high resistance to the flow of charge. Insulators are usually non-metals; metals conduct charge very easily. Since charge does not flow easily to even out, they can be charged with friction.

Question 192: A
The car accelerates for the first 10 seconds at a constant rate and then decelerates after t=30 seconds. It does not reverse, as the velocity is not negative.

Question 193: B
The distance travelled by the car is represented by the area under the curve (integral of velocity) which is given by the area of two triangles and a rectangle:
$$Area = \left(\frac{1}{2} \times 10 \times 10\right) + (20 \times 10) + \left(\frac{1}{2} \times 10 \times 10\right)$$
$$Area = 50 + 200 + 50 = 300 \, m$$
Alternatively, you can use the area for a trapezium to get the same result:
$$area = \frac{1}{2}(a+b) \times height$$

Question 194: C
Using the equation force = mass × acceleration, where the unknown acceleration = change in velocity over change in time.
Hence: $\frac{F}{m} = \frac{change\ in\ velocity}{change\ in\ time}$
We know that F = 10,000 N, mass = 1,000 kg and change in time is 5 seconds.
So, $\frac{10,000}{1,000} = \frac{change\ in\ velocity}{5}$
So change in velocity = $10 \times 5 = 50 \, m/s$

TOUGH GCSE WORKBOOK: SCIENCE — ANSWERS

Question 195: D

This question tests both your ability to convert unusual units into SI units and to select the relevant values from the information given in the question (e.g. the crane's mass is not important here).

0.01 tonnes = 10 kg; 100 cm = 1 m; 5,000 ms = 5 s

$$Power = \frac{Work\ Done}{Time} = \frac{Force \times Distance}{Time}$$

In this case the force is the weight of the wardrobe = $10 \times g = 10 \times 10 = 100N$. Thus, $Power = \frac{100 \times 1}{5} = 20\ W$

Question 196: E

Remember that the resistance of a parallel circuit (R_T) is given by:
$$\frac{1}{R_T} = \frac{1}{R_1} + \frac{1}{R_2} + \ldots$$

Thus, $\frac{1}{R_T} = \frac{1}{1} + \frac{1}{2} = \frac{3}{2}$ and therefore $R = \frac{2}{3}\ \Omega$

Using Ohm's Law: $I = \frac{20\ V}{\frac{2}{3}\ \Omega} = 20 \times \frac{3}{2} = 30$ A

Question 197: E

Water is denser than air. Therefore, the speed of light decreases when it enters water and increases when it leaves water. The direction of light also changes when light enters or leaves water in comparison to air. This phenomenon is known as refraction and is governed by Snell's Law.

TOUGH GCSE WORKBOOK: SCIENCE — ANSWERS

Question 198: C
The voltage in a parallel circuit is the same across each branch, i.e. branch A Voltage = branch B Voltage.
The resistance of Branch A = 6 x 5 = 30 Ω; the resistance of Branch B = 10 x 2 = 20 Ω.
Using Ohm's Law: I= V/R. Thus, $I_A = \frac{60}{30} = 2\,A$; $I_B = \frac{60}{20} = 3\,A$

Question 199: C
This is a very straightforward question, but it is made harder by the awkward units you have to work with. Ensure you are able to work comfortably with prefixes of 10^9 and 10^{-9} and convert to decimals without difficulty.
50,000,000,000 nano Watts = 50 W and 0.000000004 Giga Amperes = 4 A.
Using $P = IV$: $V = \frac{P}{I} = \frac{50}{4} = 12.5\,V = 0.0125\,kV$

Question 200: B
Radioactive decay is highly random and unpredictable. Only gamma decay releases gamma rays and few types of decay release X-rays. The total electrical charge of an atom's nucleus decreases after alpha decay as two protons are lost.

Question 201: D
Using $P = IV$: $I = \frac{P}{V} = \frac{60}{15} = 4\,A$
Now using Ohm's Law: $R = \frac{V}{I} = \frac{15}{4} = 3.75\,\Omega$
So, each resistor has a resistance of $\frac{3.75}{3} = 1.25\,\Omega$. If two more resistors are added, the overall resistance = 1.25 x 5 = 6.25 Ω

Question 202: E

There is not enough information to answer this question. We would be required to know the resistive forces acting against the tractor and if there is any change in height in order to calculate the useful work done and hence the efficiency.

Question 203: E

Electromagnetic induction is defined by statements 1 and 2. An electrical current is generated when a coil moves in a magnetic field.
Thus, all 3 statements are correct.

Question 204: D

An ammeter will always give the same reading in a series circuit, but it will not in a parallel circuit where the current splits at each branch in accordance with Ohm's Law.

Question 205: D

1 – **correct** – note, this is not true in parallel circuits!
2 – **correct** – the current is directed from the positive terminal towards the negative terminal.
3 – **incorrect** – electrons move in the opposite direction to current, i.e. they move from negative to positive.

Question 206: A
For a fixed resistor, the current is directly proportional to the potential difference. **This is shown in graph A.**
For a filament lamp, as current increases, the metal filament becomes hotter. This causes the metal atoms to vibrate and move more, resulting in more collisions with the flow of electrons.

This makes it harder for the electrons to move through the lamp and results in increased resistance. Therefore, the graph's gradient decreases as current increases. **This is shown in graph B.**

Question 207: D
A – correct – vectors can be added to one another, although you must take into account the direction of each vector quantity in the sum!
B – correct – all vectors are comprised of both direction and magnitude.
C – correct – see explanation for B.

All of the statements are correct, thus the correct answer to the question is **D**.

Question 208: C
The gravity on the moon is 6 times less than 10 ms^{-2}. Thus, $g_{moon} = \frac{10}{6} = \frac{5}{3}$ ms^{-2}.
Since weight = mass x gravity, the mass of the rock = $\frac{250}{\frac{5}{3}} = \frac{750}{5} = 150\ kg$
Therefore, the density = $\frac{mass}{volume} = \frac{150}{250} = 0.6\ kg/cm^3$

TOUGH GCSE WORKBOOK: SCIENCE — ANSWERS

Question 209: D
An alpha particle consists of a helium nucleus. Thus, alpha decay causes the mass number to decrease by 4 and the atomic number to decrease by 2. Five iterations of this would decrease the mass number by 20 and the atomic number by 10.

Question 210: C
Using Ohm's Law: The potential difference entering the transformer (V_1) = 10 x 20 = 200 V
Now use $\frac{N1}{N2} = \frac{V1}{V2}$ to give: $\frac{5}{10} = \frac{200}{V2}$
Thus, $V_2 = \frac{2,000}{5}$ = 400 V

Question 211: D
For objects in free fall that have reached terminal velocity, acceleration = 0.
Thus, the sphere's weight = resistive forces.
Using Work Done = Force x Distance: Force = 10,000 J/100 m = 100 N.
Therefore, the sphere's weight = 100 N and since $g = 10 ms^{-2}$, the sphere's mass = 10 kg

TOUGH GCSE WORKBOOK: SCIENCE — ANSWERS

Question 212: E
A – incorrect – the wavelength of ultraviolet waves is longer than that of x-rays.
B – incorrect – wavelength is inversely proportional to frequency.
C – incorrect – waves in the EM spectrum travel at the speed of light.
D – incorrect – humans are only able to visualise a very small part of the spectrum.
E – correct – none, of the above statements were correct, so E is the correct answer.

Question 213: B
If an object moves towards the sensor, the wavelength will appear to decrease and the frequency increase. The faster this happens, the faster the increase in frequency and decrease in wavelength.

Question 214: A
$Acceleration = \frac{Change\ in\ Velocity}{Time} = \frac{1,000}{0.1} = 10,000\ ms^{-2}$

Using Newton's second law: the braking force = Mass x Acceleration. Thus, braking force = $10,000 \times 0.005 = 50\ N$

Question 215: C
Polonium has undergone alpha decay. Thus, Y is a helium nucleus and contains 2 protons and 2 neutrons.
Therefore, 10 moles of Y contain $2 \times 10 \times 6 \times 10^{23}$ protons = $120 \times 10^{23} = 1.2 \times 10^{25}$ protons.

TOUGH GCSE WORKBOOK: SCIENCE — ANSWERS

Question 216: C
The rod's activity is less than 1,000 Bq after 300 days. In order to calculate the longest possible half-life, we must assume that the activity is just below 1,000 Bq after 300 days. Thus, the half-life has decreased activity from 16,000 Bq to 1,000 Bq in 300 days.
After one half-life: Activity = 8,000 Bq
After two half-lives: Activity = 4,000 Bq
After three half-lives: Activity = 2,000 Bq
After four half-lives: Activity = 1,000 Bq
Thus, the rod has halved its activity a minimum of 4 times in 300 days. 300/4 = 75 days

Question 217: E
There is no change in the atomic mass or proton numbers in gamma radiation. In β decay, a neutron is transformed into a proton (and an electron is released). This results in an increase in proton number by 1 but no overall change in atomic mass. Thus, after 5 rounds of beta decay, the proton number will be 89 + 5 = 94 and the mass number will remain at 200. Therefore, there are 94 protons and 200-94 = 106 neutrons.
NB: You are not expected to know about β^+ decay.

Question 218: C
Calculate the speed of the sound $= \frac{distance}{time} = \frac{500}{1.5} = 333 \; ms^{-1}$

Thus, the $Wavelength = \frac{Speed}{Frequency} = \frac{333}{440}$

Approximate 333 to 330 to give: $\frac{330}{440} = \frac{3}{4} = 0.75 \; m$

Question 219: B

Firstly, note the all the answer options are a magnitude of 10 apart. Thus, you don't have to worry about getting the correct numbers as long as you get the correct power of 10. So, you can make your life easier by rounding, e.g. approximate π to 3, etc.

The area of the shell = πr^2.
= $\pi \times (50 \times 10^{-3})^2 = \pi \times (5 \times 10^{-2})^2$
= $\pi \times 25 \times 10^{-4} = 7.5 \times 10^{-3} \, m^2$

The deceleration of the shell = $\frac{u-v}{t} = \frac{200}{500 \times 10^{-6}} = 0.4 \times 10^6 \, ms^{-2}$

Then, using Newton's Second Law: $Braking \, force = mass \times acceleration = 1 \times 0.4 \times 10^6 = 4 \times 10^5 N$

Finally: $Pressure = \frac{Force}{Area} = \frac{4 \times 10^5}{7.5 \times 10^{-3}} = \frac{8}{15} \times 10^8 \, Pa \approx 5 \times 10^7 Pa$

Question 220: B

The fountain transfers 10% of 1,000 J of energy per second into 120 litres of water per minute. Thus, it transfers 100 J into 2 litres of water per second.
Therefore, the total gravitational potential energy, $E_p = mg\Delta h$
Thus, $100 \, J = 2 \times 10 \times h$
Hence, $h = \frac{100}{20} = 5 \, m$

Question 221: E

In step down transformers, the number of turns of the primary coil is larger than that of the secondary coil to decrease the voltage. If a transformer is 100% efficient, the electrical power input = electrical power output (P=IV).

Question 222: C

The percentage of C^{14} in the bone halves every 5,730 years. Since it has decreased from 100% to 6.25%, it has undergone 4 half-lives. Thus, the bone is 4 x 5,730 years old = 22,920 years

Question 223: E

This is a straightforward question in principle, as it just requires you to plug the values into the equation: $Velocity = Wavelength \times Frequency$ – Just ensure you work in SI units to get the correct answer.
$Frequency = \frac{2\,m/s}{2.5\,m} = 0.8\,Hz = 0.8 \times 10^{-6} MHz = 8 \times 10^{-7}\,MHz$

Question 224: E

If an element has a half-life of 25 days, its count rate will be halved every 25 days.
A total of 350/25 = 14 half-lives have elapsed. Thus, the count rate has halved 14 times. Therefore, to calculate the original rate, the final count rate must be doubled 14 times = 50×2^{14}.
$2^{14} = 2^5 \times 2^5 \times 2^4$ = 32 x 32 x 16 = 16,384.
Therefore, the original count rate = 16,384 x 50 = 819,200

Question 225: D

Remember that $V = IR = \frac{P}{I}$ and $Power = \frac{Work\ Done}{Time} = \frac{Force\ x\ Distance}{Time} = Force\ x\ Velocity$;

Thus, A is derived from: $V = IR$,

B is derived from: $= \frac{P}{I}$,

C is derived from: $Voltage = \frac{Power}{Current} = \frac{Force\ x\ Velocity}{Current}$,

Since $Charge = Current\ x\ Time$, E and F are derived from:
$Voltage = \frac{Power}{Current} = \frac{Force\ x\ Distance}{Time\ x\ Current} = \frac{J}{As} = \frac{J}{C}$,

D is incorrect as Nm = J. Thus, the correct variant would be NmC^{-1}

References

1. Pashler, H., McDaniel, M., Rohrer, D., & Bjork, R. (2008). Learning styles concepts and evidence. *Psychological Science in the Public Interest, 9.*

2. Massa, L & Mayer, R. (2006). *Testing the ATI hypothesis: Should multimedia instruction accommodate verbalizer-visualizer cognitive style?.* Available: http://www.sciencedirect.com/science/article/pii/S104160 8006000331. Last accessed 24th Jun 2017.

3. Cassidy, S. (2004). *Leaning Styles: An overview of theories, models and measures.* Available: http://www.acdowd-designs.com/sfsu_860_11/LS_OverView.pdf. Last accessed 24th Jun 2017.

4. An, D., & Carr, M., Learning styles theory fails to explain learning and achievement: Recommendations for alternative approaches. *Personality and Individual Differences* (2017), Available: http://dx.doi.org/10.1016/j.paid.2017.04.050. Last accessed 21st May 2017

5. Meyer, R. E., & Anderson, R. B. (1992). The instructive animation: Helping students build connections between words and pictures in multimedia learning. *Journal of Educational Psychology, 4.*

6. Mangen, A & Velay, J. (2010). *Digitizing Literacy: Reflections on the Haptics of Writing.* Available: https://www.intechopen.com/books/advances-in-haptics/digitizing-literacy-reflections-on-the-haptics-of-writing. Last accessed 24th Jun 2017.

7. Mueller, P & Oppenheimer, D. (2014). *The Pen Is Mightier Than The Keyboard: Advantages of Longhand Over Laptop Note Taking.* Available: http://journals.sagepub.com/doi/abs/10.1177/0956797614524581. Last accessed 24th Jun 2017.

8. Cirillo Company. (.). *Pomodoro Technique.* Available: http://cirillocompany.de/pages/pomodoro-technique. Last accessed 22nd Dec 2016.

9. Chen et al. (2017). *Strategic Resource Use for Learning: A Self-Administered Intervention That Guides Self-Reflection on Effective Resource Use Enhances Academic Performance.* Available: http://journals.sagepub.com/doi/10.1177/0956797617696456. Last accessed 24th Jun 2017.

10. Larsen et al. (2013). *Comparative effects of test-enhanced learning and self-explanation on long-term retention..* Available: https://www.ncbi.nlm.nih.gov/pubmed/23746156. Last accessed 22nd Dec 2016.

11. Cepeda et al. (2006). *Distributed Practice in Verbal Recall Tasks: A Review and Quantitative Synthesis.* Available: http://www.evullab.org/pdf/CepedaPashlerVulWixtedRohrer-PB-2006.pdf. Last accessed 22nd Dec 2016.

12. Taylor & Rohrer. (2010). *The Effects of Interleaved Practice.* Available: http://uweb.cas.usf.edu/~drohrer/pdfs/Taylor&Rohrer2010ACP.pdf. Last accessed 22nd Dec 2016.

13. AcademicTips. (.). *Association, Imagination & Location.* Available: http://www.academictips.org/memory/assimloc.html. Last accessed 22nd Dec 2016.

14. Dolegui. (2013). *The Impact of Listening to Music on Cognitive Performance.* Available: http://www.inquiriesjournal.com/articles/762/2/the-impact-of-listening-to-music-on-cognitive-performance. Last accessed 22nd Dec 2016.

FINAL ADVICE

Once you have worked through these questions at least twice, and you are happy with the results you are getting, we have some last-minute tips to help ensure you perform as well as you can on the day!

Arrive well rested, well fed and well hydrated

The Science GCSEs are among the most difficult, so make sure you're ready for them. Ensure you get a good night's sleep before the exams (there is no point cramming) and don't miss breakfast. If you're taking water into the exam then make sure you've been to the toilet before so you don't have to leave during the exam. Make sure you're well rested and fed in order to be at your best!

Move on

If you're struggling, move on. In the time it takes to answer one hard question, you could gain three times the marks by answering the easier ones. Be smart to score points.

Afterword

Remember that the route to a high score is your approach and practice. Don't worry about the tough questions too much! With knowledge of the test, some useful time-saving techniques and plenty of practice you can dramatically boost your score.

Work hard, never give up and do yourself justice.
Good luck!

www.ingramcontent.com/pod-product-compliance
Lightning Source LLC
Chambersburg PA
CBHW070142100426
42743CB00013B/2798